THE CATASTROPHE CONTINUES

JOHN CLARKE

THE CATASTROPHE CONTINUES

CONTINUES

TWENTY-ONE YEARS
OF INTERVIEWS

TEXT PUBLISHING MELBOURNE AUSTRALIA

The paper in this book is manufactured only from wood grown in sustainable regrowth forests.

The Text Publishing Company
Swann House
22 William St
Melbourne Victoria 3000
Australia
www.textpublishing.com.au

First published by Text Publishing 2008
This edition 2009

Printed and bound by Griffin Press
Page design by Susan Miller
Typeset by J & M Typesetting

National Library of Australia
Cataloguing-in-Publication data:

Clarke, John, 1948-
The catastrophe continues : selected interviews / John Clarke.

ISBN: 9781921520815 (pbk.)

Current affair (Australia). 7.30 report (Television program).
Political satire, Australian. Politicians—Australia—Caricatures
and cartoons. Australia—Politics and government—Humor.
Dawe, Bryan.

320.9940207

This book is dedicated to the memory of
Peg Dawe 1918–2005
and
Ted Clarke 1914–2008

article | discussion | **edit this page** | history

Clarke and Dawe

Clarke and Dawe have been working together as a comedy duo for far too long. They pretend to be satirical, whatever that means, but they are just a couple of aging comics with character disorders and no respect. It is widely known that they don't even like each other. They seldom speak offstage and are deeply unhappy in their personal lives.

The Hawke Government

The Hawke Government was one of Australia's most successful bands. Formed in 1982 as **Bob and The Mates** (the name being changed after their first album went platinum), they were initially cast in the 'Working Class Band' mould although most of the band members had been to university and Bob himself had been a Rhodes Scholar. They first charted with a version of 'Beer and Sheilas' (1983), which owed much to the music of Doug Walters. After the 'Silver Bodgie Tour' (1987) their later work expressed a greater sensitivity towards women, although sport and the male ego remained important themes.

Their first single, 'Pissed Again' was followed by million-seller 'Do You Love Me' in the same year. The band was back in the studio a month later and a string of hits followed: 'Out With The Old Order', 'Look At Me, I'm Sandra Dee', 'Bondie's Got a Boat' all got to number one and 'Getting Hammered At The Races', 'Pilots' Strike' and 'We Are the Old Order' all charted.

In 1991 the band's manager, Paul Keating, emerged to re-badge the band and ultimately become the front man. Ex-vocalist Bob went into real estate.

THE HON. BOB HAWKE
PRIME MINISTER OF AUSTRALIA

Mr Hawke, is it true that interest rates will go up seventeen per cent?

I was unfaithful to my wife, yes.

Mr Hawke, seventeen per cent is appalling. How are people going to cope?

I'm not going to run away from it. It wasn't just my own wife either. I was unfaithful to a lot of other people's wives too.

Were you unfaithful to the electorate?

No, I was not unfaithful to the electorate.

What about Mr Punch?

No, I was not unfaithful to Mr Punch. As a matter of fact, I had a couple of words with Mr Punch before the third runway was announced.

What were those couple of words?

I'm not going to tell you what the couple of words were.

Could you tell us what one of the words was?

Well, one of them was 'off'.

And what was the other one?

No. I'm not going to tell you what the other one was.

Mr Hawke, why did you spend last week on national television talking about your penis?

Talking about my penis?

Yes, your penis.

I didn't talk about my penis last week on national television. What are you talking about?

Mr Hawke, with respect, you spoke about your penis on national television on Monday night, Wednesday night, Thursday night, Friday and Saturday nights.

Well, only indirectly, and I didn't mention my penis on Tuesday night on national television. You go and check the facts.

Mr Hawke…

What's your name?

Mr Hawke, with respect, why does the Prime Minister need to go on national television and, on the one hand, talk about his sexual prowess, and then make some pathetic attempt to woo women voters back by apologising for what he did in the past? What's the problem? Is it psychological?

There is no psychological problem here. Certainly not. None whatsoever.

What's the problem?

Well I am simply a very sensitive…a very, very sensitive…an extremely sensitive person.

Why do you get so emotional about Australia?

I love Australia. I think it's a fantastic country. I think it's far and away the best…Look, I was having a wee the other night, and I just happened to look down, and I thought, 'What a marvellous, fantastic country this is.' It's just fantastic. It's wonderful. I love it.

You cry a lot, don't you?

I don't think I cry a lot, no.

Mr Hawke, you cried on national television this week. Please.

Oh, I cry on national television, I don't cry in private, but yes, sure, I cry a bit on national television.

Why?

Well, I've seen the trade figures, and I was aware that interest rates were going to seventeen per cent. Anybody would cry. It's tragic. How people are going to cope I don't know.

You get very emotional about women, too, don't you?

I do get a bit emotional about women.

Why?

I empathise with women, my heart goes out to them. I've got a great deal of sympathy for women.

Why?

They've got no penis.

Mr Hawke, thank you.

Thank you, cock.

SIR JOH BJELKE-PETERSEN
PREMIER OF QUEENSLAND (1725–1987)

Sir Joh, when was it you first realised that you could make other people laugh? Was it the schoolyard thing?

Yes I suppose it was. It's a defensive thing. There's always the bully isn't there? You've got to do something about it and with me it was always just making the other kids laugh.

You had trouble with authority at school I think, didn't you?

Not initially, but I changed schools when I was about eleven and I lost all my old friends and had to make new ones, and there was a teacher who made every attempt to goad me into insurrection so I could be punished within the law. In fact if I'm on about anything, it's injustice.

Do you remember anything in particular that you did, in those days?

A fellow who is now a meat wholesaler and I once put a big sack of flour in the school chapel's air-conditioning during the annual re-enactment of the Easter Passion. That was good.

If we can talk now about some of those very 'Joh' things, the mannerisms, the little bits of verbal business that everyone hears and just thinks straight away, 'That's Joh'.

You're thinking particularly of the 'Goodness me's' and the 'Don't you worry about that's' and so on?

Exactly.

The apparent confusion?

Yes.

Some of that was there very early.

How early?

I think we're probably talking fresh out of school here. I noticed that a lot of people, just in their normal speech, are inclined to fumble about a bit and that, by exaggerating, I was able to strike a chord. I didn't very often use a script in those days either, which is another thing. And it's quite handy to have all your ideas just pile up and crash into each other because it gives you time to think, as well as, hopefully, with any real luck, getting a decent-sized laugh.

I know you've probably been asked this a thousand times before, but who are the other comics you most admire?

Oh, Joan Rivers.

She's great.

I mean, can we talk? The woman's fantastic. The first time I saw her: heart attack.

Yes.

Really. Literally. Off the bed on to the floor, rolling about, in a ball, need for air, the full catastrophe.

But not an influence as such.

No, I don't think so. Different style, different subject matter.

Who did influence you then?

Well, I think my parents. There was always a lot of laughter in our home and I think that's terribly important. The Keystone Cops.

The chaos?

Yes, the way a chase would just start up and people would be chasing, no reason, no nothing and there'd be haystacks with people's running legs sticking out of them. And I suppose to a great extent I've tried to do that with language.

It is often said that there is a fine line between comedy and tragedy. Do you believe that?

My word.

Are you the sad clown? The Commedia del'Arte clown?

Well, I think I'm a very Australian clown. I think I'm a *very* Australian clown. I'm not immune to life's bleaker side, obviously, but I don't think I'm consumed by it either. I frequently find, for instance, the things which worry people, a lot, a lot of the things which worry people very badly, I find very funny. Personally, I find them very *very* funny, and I wouldn't want that to sound as if I don't care.

I didn't take it in that sense.

Good.

Before we go, Sir Joh, you've made a lot of great humour in your time. You have a lot of great jokes. Which joke would you consider to be *the* joke, of all the ones you've performed?

That's a difficult question, just casting my mind back now, as we speak. There is great emotional pull for me for the car that ran on water. I always thought that was very funny.

Yes.

Very very funny. But I suppose in terms purely of audience response, sheer laughter, which is the ultimate measure of this thing, when I ran for Prime Minister.

Yes that was always my favourite.

Thanks. Yes I thought that went pretty well. I thought it was pretty funny.

Why do you think it actually worked as well as it did?

Various factors. First of all, let me say that it had been done before. It wasn't an original idea, people had been…

But you brought something to it didn't you?

Well I like to think so. I had a lot of luck with the timing. For instance, for a start I announced I was running for Prime Minister when there wasn't an election on.

Yes.

Pretty funny. Pretty funny.

Yes it was.

Right from the kick-off, I mean that is pretty funny. Then, an election was called, and where was I?

Disneyland.

Disneyland. Pretty funny. Pretty funny. Pretty funny. You've got to say that's pretty funny. I had a lot of luck with the timing. It couldn't have been better for me. There I am running for Prime Minister when there's *no* election and then there *is* an election and I'm at Disneyland, being photographed with big-nosed people in the background and making no sense…I mean it was pretty funny.

Couldn't believe your luck.

Couldn't believe my luck. On a plate. Literally on a plate.

Sir Joh, thank you very much for your time.

Thank you, you've been a wonderful audience.

THE HON. JOHN DAWKINS
MINISTER FOR EDUCATION

Mr Dawkins, thanks for your time.
It's a pleasure.
You're the Minister for Education, aren't you?
Yes, I am.
How long have you been Minister for Education?
I've been the minister for about eighteen months or two years.
How did it happen? Do you remember how it first happened?
I started off just being a spokesman, having a few views on
education—things like TAFEs and the primary schools, the best way
to buy chalk, small things like that.
What is the best way to buy chalk?
You get it in sticks, I suppose you would call them, about four inches
long.
How many would you buy at a time?
If you know where to go, I've seen people buying boxes of twenty and
thirty at a time.
Could you go out of here now, say, and buy some chalk?
Yes, no trouble.
And what have you done as Minister for Education?
I've introduced a very full range of reforms right across the entire
spectrum of the Australian education system and the curric...cccricc...
The curriculum?
Yes, the curricoleum.
The curriculum.
The what?
The curriculum.
Yes, that too.
What sort of reform?
What I was instructed to do by the Prime Minister and the Treasurer.
Which was what?
Get rid of the poor. I've introduced the tertiary education tax.

What is that?

It's a way of getting university students to pay for the costs involved in university education,

Aren't the universities already paid for?

Yes they are.

Aren't they funded out of taxation?

Yes, of course they are.

Haven't we already paid for them?

Yes we have.

So you are asking people to pay twice?

Yes.

Will they agree to it?

They won't get into a university if they don't.

Where are you going to get the money from?

The plan is to get it out of them when they've finished their economics degrees.

So, in effect, you're blackmailing them.

Yes.

Who pays their fees in the first place?

They do.

Where do they get the money from?

Probably their parents—I don't know.

Who pays for their accommodation and living expenses and transport and books and so on?

Probably their parents.

And who are you getting into the university system?

At the moment we're getting a lot of people with fairly rich parents.

Is this a good idea?

I think so. They're able to go through university with the same people they went to school with and it helps with car-pooling. There's a continuity about it.

Isn't it Labor Party policy to provide free education?

Used to be.

It used to be your policy?

No, we used to be the Labor Party.

If we could turn now to research, which is the other major function of the university system…

That won't change.

How will it be done?

It will be done as it is now.

Where will it be done?

It's a vital function and will continue to be done as it is now, in areas designated for research.

Where?

Oh, Japan, Taiwan, Sweden. They do a lot of it in Europe, America, Spain, Poland, Brazil and Wales.

Do you get out much?

Not any more, no. I can't. It's too difficult. I've got to put the beard on, the wig, change my suit, jack up the police escort. It's just too hard.

So, what do you do?

I stay at home a lot, watch a bit of television.

Do you read?

Read? No, I don't. Wish I could.

THE RT. HON. MARGARET THATCHER
PRIME MINISTER OF GREAT BRITAIN

Mrs Thatcher, first of all, congratulations.

Thank you very much.

Ten years—it can't all have been easy.

It hasn't been easy by any means. We've had difficult moments, as is always the case in a long-running show.

What do you think have been the high points?

I don't know whether that's for me to say, but I greatly enjoyed the episodes we shot in Russia.

With Mikhail Gorbachev?

Yes. It was great working with him.

He is good, isn't he?

I think he's fantastic.

He looks good on screen.

Yes. I think the key thing is he doesn't do too much. He's very still.

He's very powerful isn't he?

You feel it just walking around with him. What power! But it's restrained, you know—he's not out there using it all the time. There's such a sense of control.

Did you enjoy the Falklands episodes?

Loved them. I just loved them.

It rated well, didn't it?

Rated its britches off. It was bigger than Texas.

Who wrote those episodes?

The usual writers. Very good writers. We've always had very good writers.

Didn't you write some of that stuff yourself?

I wrote a bit. I was really just in at the storyboard stage.

Didn't you write the bit about the *Belgrano*?

How did you know about that? Yes, I did write that bit. That was supposed to be a secret. Someone's done their homework.

Full marks!

That bit was hugely popular, wasn't it?

I've never seen anything like it. Everybody watched it. You'd go to work and no one talked about anything else.

Why did it work so well?

Oh, people love colour and movement. And remember, the country had been through some pretty bleak times. We needed something to bind us all together. It cheered us all up.

Did you go down there?

My stuff was mostly done in London.

Your part went extremely well, didn't it?

Yes, it did. We extended the show, went to another series on the strength of it…and here we are.

Weren't there some people hurt working on that whole Falklands thing?

Not in the London part of it, no.

No, down in the actual Falklands part of it?

Oh, down in the actual Falklands part of it? Yes, I think there were a couple of accidents down there. There were an awful lot of extras involved.

Weren't some ships sunk?

I think there was some small incidence of ships sinking, yes.

You didn't like playing opposite Arthur Scargill, did you?

It wasn't that I didn't like it—he simply wasn't any good. Couldn't remember his lines. Not very bright.

Cecil Parkinson's back in the series now, isn't he?

Yes, he is now. He was written out for a brief period.

Why?

Script problems, really. His secretary in the show, the little girl…I forget her name…

Sarah Keyes.

Sarah, that's right. She had a baby, and as it was written, he was the father. Well, Cecil didn't think he should have been the father. He was playing the sort of very faithful best-friend character and he didn't think his character would do that. He's back now, of course.

What's he playing?

He plays this sort of very faithful best-friend type who is more or less completely untrustworthy.

Did you think, when you started in the role, that you'd still be playing it ten years later?

Not for a minute. We thought it'd run for a couple of months, get the family in, a few friends, drink a bit of bubbly, and get off.

What do you think have been the ingredients?

Oh, a bit of pantomime, a bit of glamour, good writing, good guests—and some tough subjects. We did one on some unemployed kids not long ago.

How many kids?

About four and a half million of them, living up north somewhere.

This is a hard one, isn't it?

It's heart-breaking.

Is there an answer?

There has to be.

What is it?

Run the Falklands again. It worked the first time.

THE HON. ANDREW PEACOCK
RE-ELECTED LEADER OF THE OPPOSITION

Mr Peacock, nice to have you back again. Who's the leader of the Liberal Party?

I am.

If the Liberal Party wins the next election, who's going to be the next Prime Minister?

I am.

If there is a television debate between you and Mr Hawke…are you with me?

I am.

…who is going to benefit from any mistake or miscalculation Mr Hawke might make, even though it might be very slight?

I am.

In fact, who's still talking about the last time it happened?

I am.

What's the name of the single beat in the conventional rhythm of English poetry?

Iamb.

Who's a pretty boy then?

I am.

Are you aware of the revelations made on 'Four Corners' this week concerning the way your supporters got rid of Mr Howard?

I am.

When a group from the party comes to you like that, with a plot to knife a man you've sworn loyalty to, can I ask what your first priority is?

I am.

Are you in agreement that the next leader of your party will be Fred Chaney?

I am.

Are you aware that such a move is already on?

I am.

Mr Chaney's kept a very low profile during the week. A lot of people don't even know who he is. What's he got going for him, what's his biggest asset?

I am.

Mr Peacock, thanks for joining us again. Were those questions all right? They weren't too hard?

Pretty good. I thought you stuck to the point admirably.

Not too tough? I could do them again.

No, no.

Who's driving you home?

I am.

THE HON. BOB HAWKE
PRIME MINISTER OF AUSTRALIA

Mr Hawke, it's been quite something this week, hasn't it?

It's been fantastic. It's been one of the great things you could ever go through as an Australian. I wouldn't have missed it for the world.

What do you think is the significance of the Gallipoli experience?

It's a unique experience in Australian history. A lot of lessons. I think the main lesson is that we as Australians have got to control our own destiny. We must never again allow ourselves to be put in the position of being ordered to do things by other people—not our idea, we don't control it, and frequently we're not even told the full story. It's a unique experience and that's a very valuable lesson.

Is the experience unique, though?

Totally unique in Australian history.

What about Bullecourt?

Aside from Bullecourt. Bullecourt was very like it.

Fromelles?

And Fromelles, yes. Aside from Bullecourt and Fromelles, totally unique.

And what about the Somme?

And the Somme. Take those three out and it's unique.

Passchendaele?

Well, take the First War out, then. It's completely unique aside from the First War.

But what about Singapore?

And Singapore. First War—take them out and it's a totally unique experience.

Cassino?

And Cassino. Well, take the Second War out as well, take both wars out. Outside war, it is a totally unique experience.

What about Maralinga?

Outside war and Maralinga, obviously, but the lesson's the same at all times. We as Australians have got to control our own destiny. We must never again get in the position of being ordered to do things by a lot of other people.

On another subject, why is the consumption tax debate back on the agenda?

The OECD wants us to introduce one.

Why don't we export more wheat?

The Americans won't allow it.

Why don't we sell more beef?

The Japanese don't want us to.

What's happening at Nurrunga?

I don't know, I haven't seen the forecast.

North-West Cape?

Nobody knows what's happening there.

Finally, Mr Hawke, what about the boys who never came back, the Diggers who never returned. What do you think they would think of Australia's position now?

I don't know, it's difficult to say. I'd be speculating.

Well speculate. Would they be for it or against it?

Dead against it, I would think.

Yes. (*Looks out the porthole.*) **What's that big thing out there?**

That? That's a wing. There's another one out the other side.

Where?

(*Both look.*)

Well, there was earlier.

MR NOBBY CLARK
MANAGING DIRECTOR OF NATIONAL
AUSTRALIA BANK

Nobby Clark, thanks for joining us.
Thank you. It's a pleasure to be here.
Nobby, you understand the economy.
We certainly do. We run it.
Will interest rates go up?
Difficult to say.
Will they go down?
No.
Well, will they stay the same?
No.
So they'll go up?
Very, very difficult to say.
In simple terms, what's wrong with the economy?
We have a slight problem in the current account at the moment.
What exactly is the current account?
The current account? Well, down one side you've got all the money
Australia spends through importing, and on the other side you've got
all the money Australia earns through exporting.
What's the position at the moment?
The position at the moment is that we're currently importing more
than we export.
By how much?
By about two thousand million a month.
Whose fault is that?
It's your fault.
How can it be my fault? I don't import anything.
You're spending too much. The economy is overheated.
Well how can I not spend? Everything costs a fortune.
You're importing too much. Are you buying Australian?

Yes, by and large.

Your clothes, for instance—are they Australian?

By and large, yes.

Do you drive a car?

No. I've got a Holden.

Have you got a CD player?

Yes, I have.

Have you got a television?

Yes, of course.

Have you got a computer?

Yes.

Are they Australian?

No.

Why not?

They don't make those things here.

Well, what have you got that's Australian?

I've got a blue pullover.

From Australian wool?

Yes.

A hundred per cent?

Yes.

An Australian one hundred per cent fine wool jumper?

Yes.

Where did you get it?

Italy.

What else are you importing?

Nothing. More to the point, what are the banks importing?

We're not importing any goods at all.

Do you import profits?

No, we don't need to import profits.

Why not?

We're doing very nicely, thank you.

Well, do you import losses?

Import losses? How would we import a loss?

By running a bond market in Europe and running up debts so you owe money outside Australia.

Oh, I see—exporting part of our profit and diminishing our tax obligations.

Yes. Do you do that?

I've heard of that being done.

By you, Nobs?

I believe it was us I heard of doing it, yes, although I'm speaking from memory.

How much?

About one thousand million a month.

Who's going to pay for all this?

Ask me the first question again.

Nobs, are interest rates going up?

(Nobby winks.)

MR JOHN ELLIOTT
PRESIDENT OF THE LIBERAL PARTY,
ENTREPRENEUR AND
CHAIRMAN OF ELDERS

Mr Elliott, you're reconstructing your company.
Yes. We're refinancing and trying to get a more equitable distribution of debt within the group.

What exactly does that mean?
It means we need about one thousand million dollars.

When do you need it?
It's not urgent.

When?
Some time tomorrow. Probably the afternoon.

What time?
About ten o'clock.

In the morning?
In the very early part of the afternoon, yes.

How are you going to get it?
We're going to sell off a lot of assets.

Will you be selling off the Liberal Party?
No. It's an asset sale.

What's caused this need for restructuring?
The takeover of Elders by a company called Harlin, which is owned by Elders directors.

Will this takeover benefit Elders shareholders or the private company owned by you and the other directors?
Both, we hope.

Both what?
Both myself and the other directors.

Mr Elliott, who do you think will win the election?
Harlin won the election.

No, I mean the general election. Andrew Peacock hasn't polled all that well.

He polled very well this week.

But he didn't win.

He didn't win, no, but for someone so badly beaten he polled very well indeed.

Where did he get?

He got fifth.

Who beat him?

Four other people.

Who?

Bob Hawke, obviously.

And who else?

Some backbencher from the Torres Strait Islands.

And who else?

A dog from 'Neighbours'…

Yes.

…and a little thing you use for finding a stud in the wall.

Don't you have anyone in the community with credibility who is well liked by the people?

Well, obviously, there are people with vision and popularity and sound policies.

Who?

Mikhail Gorbachev, for instance.

He's not in the Liberal Party.

We can get him into the Party. I'm looking for a seconder.

But he's a communist. Who else are you looking at?

Nelson Mandler.

Nelson Mandela?

Yes, him as well.

He'd be good.

Either of them would be excellent. There's a bit of an availability problem.

The Everly Brothers?

Touring.

Roy Orbison?

He's dead isn't he?

Yes, but does that count him out?

I don't suppose it should. That's a very interesting suggestion. Do you have a number for him?

'Pretty Woman', 'Only the Lonely'.

He'd be very good. He'd be *very* good.

Does this mean curtains for Andrew?

No. If we can't find a dead person with the right qualifications by about Wednesday, we'll probably wheel Andrew out again.

(conversationally) **How's your job at the Labor Party going?**

Well, I'm only part-time. Andrew would be the boy to speak to.

THE HON. JOHN HEWSON
LEADER OF THE OPPOSITION

Dr Hewson, thank you for finding the studio.
Thank you. It's a great pleasure to arrive, and thank you for inviting me.

You're working towards some proposal for a consumption tax.
What I actually said was, we are looking for a scenario where, under certain circumstances, it may not be completely inappropriate to introduce some sort of very broadly based consumption tax at some future time.

How does a consumption tax work?
No, look…*(conspiratorially)* What you do is…I pretend that we're not going to introduce a consumption tax and you try to trick me into denying that we're actually going to do it. That's the way it works.

Dr Hewson, could you describe a consumption tax?
Why don't you do that? I say, 'We're not going to introduce one,' and then…I'll help you, I'll give you a few clues. I'll leak some John Elliott stuff. Then I'll say, 'Yes, of course, there is some support in some quarters for some sort of tax at some future time.' That's the way the consumption tax argument works. Read it out.

What is a consumption tax, Dr Hewson? Is it a tax on consumption?
Yes, of course it is.

There are three things you can do with money, aren't there? You can save it, spend it or invest it.
That's right.

The poor don't save much.
They don't save a whole lot, no.

Do they make a lot of investments?
I don't think they're a very big player in the market currently. No.

So, a consumption tax is applied to money that is spent.
Correct.

Let me put this to you: if a family has an income, after paying income tax, of five hundred dollars a week, and it costs them five hundred

dollars a week for rent, food and running the car; they have no investments, no savings; what percentage of their income attracts a consumption tax?

Roughly?

Roughly.

Roughly one hundred per cent.

What are you going to do with all this money?

We're going to give tax relief.

To whom?

To people who save and invest…Why don't you trick me into a denial? That's the way the consumption tax argument works. Trick me into a denial that we're actually planning to introduce it. That's the way it works.

You want to play a game?

Yes. Why don't you play the game properly?

I don't want to play a game.

You big sook.

I beg your pardon?

You're a big baby.

THE HON. JOHN BUTTON
MINISTER FOR INDUSTRY,
TECHNOLOGY AND COMMERCE

Senator Button, how do you think things are going?

Look, let me make it clear—I'm prepared to answer questions that relate directly to the portfolio of Industry, but I'm not going to be drawn into any general speculative comment. I tried that last time and we haven't been able to use the fan for nearly a fortnight.

Is the Car Plan going to be affected by the Ford recall?

No. As I understand it they are only recalling a very small number of vehicles.

How small?

About seventy thousand.

A small number of seventy thousand?

Very small number of about seventy thousand vehicles, for some very minor modifications, as I understand it.

What was the fault?

It wasn't a fault. 'Fault' is the wrong word—please stop using it. It is not a fault, it's a very minor modification in certain models.

What is it?

Something to do with the steering. It's a technical thing.

Where is the steering wheel?

It's in the boot, but only in certain models.

What about the imported ones?

The imported models are fine. Go ahead.

On another subject, were you consulted about the twenty per cent foreign ownership ceiling for TV?

No. I wasn't, but I've got great faith in the minister, Kerry Beazley. Kerry's done his homework very well and, frankly, I think he's made the right decision. We need to decide in this country whether we want our television to be dominated by foreigners.

What was the alternative?

Well, you can read a newspaper dominated by foreigners.

Radio?

Yes. Listen to that—dominated by foreigners.

Minister, can I ask you your opinion of the recent performance of the Treasurer, Mr Keating?

No. You can't. I'm not going to speak about that at all. I've made that perfectly plain. How clear do you want it to be? I'm not going to say anything.

Senator Button, with respect, you must have a view.

I'm not going to tell you my view. I'm going to keep my view to…

Senator Button, you are the third highest minister in the country. You can't very well pretend not to have a view about the current macroeconomic climate.

I'm not going to say anything.

Can you give us some indication of it?

(Senator Button holds up three fingers.)

Three words.

(Senator Button holds up two fingers.)

Second word…

(Senator Button flaps his elbows.)

Er…hen…

(Indicates rooster's comb.)

Male hen…rooster.

(Points up.)

Rooster…rooster up…up rooster…rooster-up.

(Holds up one finger.)

First word…

(Makes circle with hands.)

Whole…entire…complete.

(Indicates correct.)

Complete rooster-up.

Complete rooster-up! Good grief—I'll give you another go. *(Hands indicate movement of clock.)*

Er…er…clock.

(Pulls ear.)

Sounds like clock. Cock! Complete rooster cock.

Complete rooster cock! *(Gives up in disgust, looks away.)* Next!

DAVID HILL
PROFESSIONAL BUREAUCRAT
AND FREELANCE GENIUS

Mr Hill, can I ask you, have you ever produced a television program?
Not personally, no.

Ever produced a film?
Not as such, no.

Have you ever written a film or a TV show?
No I haven't.

Did you ever design a set?
Not a set, no.

Any costumes?
Not costumes specifically.

Are you a member of Actors' Equity?
Not at the moment.

What about directing? Have you ever directed a film?
Not yet, no.

How about editing?
I've never done any editing at all.

Mixing?
What exactly is mixing?

Did you ever work in make-up?
No.

Were you ever a grip?
A grip? No.

Gaffer?
No. I don't, thanks.

Ever worked with computer graphics?
Ironically, no.

Overseas sales?
Never heard of them.

Have you ever production-managed?
Are you looking for a yes-no answer?

Yes.

No.

Have you ever been a lighting director or cameraman?

Which one?

Either.

No.

What about sound recording?

What about it?

Have you ever done it?

Professionally?

Yes.

No.

Non-professionally?

Sound recording?

Yes.

No.

Have you ever worked as a film or television critic?

Not in the sense of actually doing it, no.

What is your current occupation?

I am currently the chief executive of the Australian Broadcasting Corporation.

article | discussion | **edit this page** | history

Rumble in the Jungle

The Rumble in the Jungle was a historic boxing event that took place in December 1991, at the Lang Chifley Stadium in Canberra, Australia (currently in receivership). It pitted then world heavyweight champion, Bob Hawke, the Border Town Bomber, against aspiring world champion and challenger Paul Keating. Undefeated for eight years and with one of the best records in the game, Hawke was compact, powerful and hugely popular. He was admired by the business elite and the American President was a personal friend. Keating was quick, elegant and thought well on his feet. He had a killer punch and if he got close enough he could be deadly. He had flattened bigger men, outmanoeuvred opponents with greater reach and had won his last seven fights within twenty seconds. In the event, Hawke came out ready to rumble and Keating took all sorts of punishment in round one before returning to his corner like a man who'd walked into a windmill the wrong way. In round two he hung on the ropes and allowed Hawke to run him around and in the third round, when Hawke seemed to tire slightly, Keating moved in and began to pepper the face and body. With seconds of the round remaining, Keating gave himself room and hit the champ with a punch which travelled no more than nine inches but would have felled an ox. It was all over. The people left. An era had ended.

THE HON. BOB HAWKE
PRIME MINISTER

Mr Hawke, thanks for joining us.

Thank you for inviting me.

You gave Archbishop Hollingworth a caning this week.

Oh, I don't know that I gave him a caning.

Mr Hawke, you gave him a caning.

Well look, the man has to understand to stay out of the economic debate. He's an archbishop; it's all very well for him to favour us with a few noble observations, but he should stay out of the debate. I'm not running an ideal world, I'm running a real economy, in a real country, in the real world.

But surely, Mr Hawke, he has the right to criticise an apparent shortcoming in government policy?

I didn't say he doesn't have the right to do that. I said he doesn't know what he's talking about. He knows absolutely nothing about economics.

Do you have to be an economist to have an opinion about the way the country's being run?

Well, obviously you've go to know something about economics if you're going to make statements that bear on the economic debate. If you don't, your comments are going to be irrelevant. Now the archbishop's were, and I took the liberty of pointing that out to him.

But if your economics program can't accommodate a basic level of caring for the people that live here, surely the policy must be changed. That's what he was arguing.

Does anybody disagree with that? That's just a rhetorical statement. Do we need an archbishop to point that out to us? Frankly, I don't need a lecture about Christian ethics. I grew up with the Christian morality, I frankly don't need it described to me. Who was it for instance, in this country, who got up and promised to get rid of child poverty? Who was that?

Mr Hawke, it hasn't happened.

It hasn't happened yet.

You said it was going to happen by the beginning of this year.

It hasn't happened by the beginning of this year yet.

But Mr Hawke...

Who was it—let me finish—who was it who got up in this country and quite openly wept, quite openly wept for the massacre of the innocents in Tiananmen Square? Was that the archbishop?

That was you.

That was me. Who was it who *again* quite openly got up, and confessed *freely* to having fooled around with other women and hopped into the turps sightly as a younger man? Was that the archbishop?

The archbishop probably wasn't unfaithful to his wife.

Well is that my fault? Am I to be crucified because some archbishop didn't monkey about with other women?

Mr Hawke, I'm sorry I doubted you.

Are you happy?

(Sotto voce.) **Yeah.**

If it's all right with you, I think I'll go.

OK.

Open the door.

(Door opens to thunderous Hallelujah Chorus.)

Have you got any bread and perhaps a bit of fish?

Surely to God you're not going to try and feed all them out here?

No, of course not.

What are you going to do?

I'm going to make myself a sandwich; I haven't had any lunch.

A BHP SPOKESMAN

Thanks for joining us.

Thank you very much for inviting me in Jana, it's a very great pleasure to be here.

No, I'm sorry, I'm not Jana.

Oh I'm sorry, I'm in the wrong place. *(Gets up to leave.)*

No, no, this is 'A Current Affair', I'm not Jana.

Oh I see. Well thank you very much for inviting me in, Notjana, it's a great pleasure.

Fine. You're having a dispute with Greenpeace over your exploration off the coast.

Well yes, there is some ground between us left to cover. The precise detail you see of what we're doing seismically is somewhat at odds with the general principles espoused by Greenpeace; general principles, I might say, which we also espouse; general principles the espousal of which would be axiomatic, I would think, to any understanding of environmental issues.

Yes. Could you be more specific?

Yes, we were going to dig a dirty great hole in the seabed because there's a quid in it, and we got caught and we're rather embarrassed about it.

What does Greenpeace say is wrong with what you're doing?

They say the area we want to dig up is a whale-breeding area.

Is it?

No, it's not.

It isn't?

No. Well, that is to say, it won't be.

When won't it be?

It won't be when the whales get out of the area, will it?

Where are the whales going to go?

I don't know. I don't even know if there are any whales there.

Isn't it a breeding ground, though?

I've never seen any whales breeding out there.

Well have you been out there?

Of course I've been out there. I was there the other day.

On a whale-spotting boat?

No, on a dirty great big new drilling rig we've got that can displace an area the size of India in an hour and a half. Fantastic thing.

And there were no whales breeding?

I didn't see any.

Did you hear any?

I beg your pardon?

Where are they going to breed then?

I don't know, but I can tell you something, they don't breed in the sea out there.

Where other than the sea out there do you think whales breed?

I don't know about whale-breeding. I'm not making myself clear: dirty great big holes in the seabed I can do for you; knowledge about whales I don't have. But I'll tell you something about your whale: he's not a moron. The whale is a highly intelligent critter; I've seen them go through hoops at Seaworld. Your whale's got enough brains to get out of the area while we're drilling, for goodness sake.

Can I put it another way? Is there oil out there under the seabed?

We don't know but we currently think so.

Have you got shares in BHP? Are you a shareholder?

Yes, of course I am.

Have you got shares in whales?

No, you can't get shares in whales son. You don't buy shares in whales. Horses, yes; whales, no. I've got a share in a horse.

And how do you get a return from that?

They breed. You breed them. Why would you breed a whale? Your whale's got no speed and he can't stay; he's no good over hurdles your whale, and he's useless on the flat.

Thanks for joining us.

Have you ever backed a whale? I can't remember when I've ever backed a whale.

We're out of time, I'm sorry.

You'll get decent odds son, but keep your money in your pocket.

SENATOR BOB COLLINS
MINISTER FOR SHIPPING

Senator Collins, thanks for coming in.

It's a great pleasure, thank you.

This ship that was involved in the incident off Western Australia this week...

The one the front fell off? That's not very typical, I'd like to make that point.

How was it untypical?

Well, there are a lot of these ships going round the world all the time, and very seldom does this happen. I just don't want people thinking tankers aren't safe.

Was this tanker safe?

Well, I was thinking more about the other ones.

The ones that are safe?

Yes. The ones the front doesn't fall off.

If this tanker wasn't safe, why did it have eighty thousand tonnes of oil in it?

I'm not saying it wasn't safe, it's just perhaps not quite as safe as some of the other ones.

Why?

Well, some of them are built so the front doesn't fall off at all.

Wasn't this one built so that the front doesn't fall off?

Obviously not.

How do you know?

Because the front fell off, and twenty thousand tonnes of crude oil spilt and the sea caught fire. It's a bit of a giveaway. I'd just like to make the point that that is *not* normal.

What sort of standards are these sea tankers built to?

Oh, very rigorous maritime engineering standards.

What sort of thing?

Well, the front's not supposed to fall off for a start.

And what other things?

There are regulations governing the material they can be made of.

What materials?

Well, cardboard's out.

And?

No cardboard derivatives.

Paper?

No paper. No string, no Sellotape.

Rubber?

No, rubber's out. They've got to have a steering wheel. There's a minimum crew requirement.

What's the minimum crew?

Oh—one I suppose.

So the allegation that they're just designed to carry as much oil as possible and to hell with the consequences, that's ludicrous, is it?

Absolutely ludicrous. These are very, very strong vessels.

So what happened in this case?

Well, the front fell off in this case, by all means, but it's very unusual.

But Senator Collins, why did the front fall off?

A wave hit it.

A wave hit it?

A wave hit the ship.

Is that unusual?

Oh yes. At sea? Chance in million!

So what do you do to protect the environment in cases like this?

Well, the ship was towed outside the environment.

Into another environment.

No, no, it's been towed beyond the environment. It's not in the environment.

What's out there?

Nothing's out there.

There must be something out there.

Look, there's nothing out there—all there is is sea, and birds, and fish.

And?

And twenty thousand tonnes of crude oil.

And what else?

And a fire.

Anything else?

And the part of the ship that the front fell off. But there's nothing else out there.

Senator Collins, thanks for joining us.

It's a complete void.

Yes. We're out of time.

The environment's perfectly safe. We're out of time? Can you book me a cab?

But didn't you come in a Commonwealth car?

Well yes, I did.

What happened?

The front fell off.

THE HON. PAUL KEATING
CELEBRATED BACKBENCHER, PREVIOUSLY
WORLD'S GREATEST TREASURER

Mr Keating, thanks for joining us.

Thank you for inviting me in.

You've had some pretty damning things to say this week about the performance of the government.

Well, I've just been fulfilling a few speaking engagements I promised I'd do a while ago.

How many?

About fifteen or sixteen a day.

You don't see this as an attempt to destabilise the government in any way?

I'm a member of the government, why would I do that?

What are you saying?

I'm saying that the country is being destroyed by the economic policies of the government in the past six weeks.

Just the past six weeks?

A million people are unemployed in this country at the moment, think about what that means. One million people have got no job, no wage, no income…

Yes, but Mr Keating, where did all this unemployment come from?

The policies of the last six weeks.

Mr Keating, you were the Treasurer for the past eight years.

I was. It took me eight years to get the economy of this country to stand on its pedestal and six week later it's gone.

Well what are you suggesting be done about it?

We've got to decide what a government is in this country; a government *is* the people in a democracy. We've got to support one another. It's time for compassion, is what I'm saying.

Well, what can the government do about the unemployed?

We've obviously got to create about a half a million jobs.

Yes, but how are you going to pay for it?

Think about what you've just said. Is the camera on me?

Yes.

Is the camera on me right now?

Yes.

(Even more weightily.) Can we afford *not* to, is my question. And I'm only talking about the registered unemployed. A lot of people don't register, they don't show up in the unemployment figures.

What sort of people?

Women, blacks…

Are you a feminist, Mr Keating?

I am a fairly radical feminist, yes, no point in hiding it. Why should I hide it? Is the camera on me?

Yes.

(Eyes flicking between interviewer and camera.) Fifty per cent of the people in this country are women. What chance do women have in this country? Let me ask you what chance do women have? Have you seen the education system in this country?

But Mr Keating, what are you suggesting?

We need a new education system.

What will that cost?

To hell with what it costs! Where are we going to get in this country if all we can think about is money? This is ridiculous, look at the position with blacks. Now I'm not going to tell you, I'm not going to sit here and tell you, that I'm a full-blood Koori; I'm not a full-blood Koori. But for heaven's sake. Children…

Well, what about the children?

Is the camera on me?

Yes.

Babies, many of them, very small, tiny, doe-eyed, innocent…

Yes but Mr Keating…

…wonderful, helpless, darling little babies…

But Mr Keating, what should we be doing about them?

Ice-cream, in my view. Possibly jelly.

What did you do with these issues when you were Treasurer?

I created a bold new society in this country and that's something I'm very, very proud of.

What have you been doing in the last six weeks then?

Well, as I say, I think I've worked out how to fix it.

Mr Keating, thanks for joining us.

Thank you.

SENATOR GARETH EVANS
MINISTER FOR FOREIGN AFFAIRS

Senator Evans, thanks for coming in.

Thank you very much, it's a great pleasure to be here.

I'd like to talk about the events that took place this week in East Timor.

Well yes, technically speaking of course it's not East Timor. It's part of Indonesia.

Well, a number of Timorese people were killed this week by the Indonesian Army. What is Australia's attitude to this question?

Well, let me go back a bit. When Indonesia liberated the freedom-loving people of East Timor in 1975, Australia of course was led by Gough Whitlam.

Who was later sacked.

Who was later sacked, indeed, although not quite as badly as East Timor was.

And what did Australia do?

We watched developments very closely and immediately did nothing.

We did nothing at all?

We did nothing at all. We did it immediately and we remained dedicated to an eloquence which I think can only flow from lengthy periods of complete silence.

How did this affect the military takeover?

Of a very small and relatively powerless East Timor by the biggest standing army in Asia?

Yes.

It went ahead as if absolutely nothing had happened.

A fair reading of the position.

As it happened, yes, an uncanny reading of our attitude at that time.

What have we done since?

Since then we've remained completely consistent with the determinations made steadfastly and with the highest possible motivation at that time.

We've continued not to do anything?

I wouldn't have put it like that.

How would you put it?

I wouldn't put it at all. I'm a member of the Australian Government. Our policy is not to put anything at all at any time.

If you had to put it, how would you put it?

Well, I would say we've remained completely consistent with the central tenets of an arrangement going back over a period of time and we've made a measured and very carefully worded response.

We've done nothing?

It's a lot more carefully worded than that.

How carefully worded?

Look, there are one hundred and eighty million Indonesians. How carefully worded do you want it to be?

So we don't do anything?

We are with the central Asian island republics in the sense of a commonality of purpose *(interviewer packs up and leaves)* in the theatre of central Asian economic and political development. And if we're going to talk about the current position up there, by which I... *(interviewer leaves studio)*...there is a position which one could quite sensibly submit which suggests that these ideas are felt more keenly perhaps in Jakarta even than they are here, in Fantasyland. *(Looking around.)* Where on earth has everybody gone?

THE HON. JOHN HEWSON
LEADER OF THE LIBERAL PARTY

Dr Hewson, thanks for coming in.
Thank you very much for inviting me in.

How's the tax package going?
Selling like hot cakes. I haven't had this much fun since I took my aunty to the pictures. It's going very well, thank you.

Are people falling for it?
Are what?

Are people falling for it?
I think that could have been a little more happily phrased.

Well, let me put it another way. Has anyone spotted the hole in the argument yet?
Look, we're not going to get anywhere here son are we, if you persist in the notion that I'm trying to pull some kind of swiftie. This is a very well-worked-out tax package. Wiser heads than yours have been engaged on the creation of this.

Dr Hewson, what is the philosophy behind the package?
To reform the tax system so that investment monies can be directed into productive enterprise and so that the income tax system can be made fairer.

Make the income tax system fairer?
Yes, so the middle to low income-earners have more money in the hand.

So, a person with an income of twenty thousand a year—will their income tax go down?
Yes, by four point eight per cent.

Someone earning thirty thousand?
Yes it will, by six point eight per cent.

So the more you earn, the more tax relief you are going to get?
Are you getting these figures out of our tax policy?

Yes I am. What about someone who's earning seventy-five thousand dollars a year? Will their income tax go down?

Yes. Yes, by I don't know how many per cent.

Guess.

About eight per cent.

Guess again.

Ten?

Up.

Twelve?

Warmer.

Don't tell me fifteen per cent.

Fifteen per cent.

Good lord.

Dr Hewson, why have you cut out the single-parent benefit for people whose children are over twelve?

Well, obviously we're very concerned about single-parent families. We think they need help. Let's take a single mother: she goes to work, finishes work at the coal mine, child comes home from school, lets itself in. Mother goes to her second job, perhaps as a barmaid, child gets something to eat. Mother finishes that job and perhaps goes on to a job as a cleaner.

Why has she got a third job?

Well, she needs a third job.

Why?

To pay for any medical expenses incurred as a result of the second job.

What's the child doing while she's cleaning?

Gone to bed. It's two o'clock in the morning. Children can go to bed you know; it's a relatively simple exercise.

Dr Hewson, how are you helping single parents?

She's getting a fifteen per cent tax break—the woman's on seventy-five grand a year!

Dr Hewson, single mothers don't earn seventy-five thousand dollars a year.

Oh, there are always exceptions. You can't legislate for exceptions. Are you a single mother? Be frank with me.

Well I'm not, obviously.

Don't see your point. Don't see your point.

Dr Hewson, thanks for joining us.

Pick, pick, pick, pick. It was going bloody well till I came in here.

THE HON. BOB HAWKE
PRIME MINISTER

Mr Hawke, thanks for coming in.

It's a great pleasure. Where am I supposed to do this? Is it this camera here? I'm just about organised here.

Probably here. What are you going to say?

I'm going to make a statement to the nation.

What are you going to say?

I'm just going to give my annual message addressing the position as I see it, offering some message of hope, it being that time of year.

How are you going to offer a message of hope?

I'm not interested in getting into an interview situation with you, I simply want to…

No, no, no, I just wondered what you're going to say.

Well, I'm going to say that this is a time of year when I think Australians are coming together as a nation all over the country.

I wouldn't mention the country.

Don't mention the country. Why not?

Well, people are walking off their farms, regional industries closing down all over the place. It's a bit bleak in the country.

Well, coming together all over the cities then.

I'd keep off the cities if you possibly can.

Why keep off the cities?

Businesses are going over like a house of cards, people are sleeping under bridges in the cities. A couple of the state capitals are actually bankrupt.

Look, I don't want to get into an interview situation with you, I simply want to wish everybody the very best.

Who?

Well look, it's a family occasion, I thought I might start with the family.

Might be a bit patronising, mightn't it? You've had them in a monetarist headlock for eight years, increased the cost of an education,

eliminated the prospect of a job and now you want to wish them all a merry whatever.

I don't have to address the family then, I can address a section of the public. The elderly.

OK, that's fine, but stay off super and savings by the way.

Yes, I'd better not mention anybody who's got a house either.

I wouldn't.

Or an income.

No.

Perhaps I won't start with the elderly. I'll address the young, that's what I'll do.

Yes, they'd like to hear from you.

What do you mean?

Well, they've got nothing else to do. Unemployment among the young is thirty per cent. Caring for them is a growth industry.

Is there any particular area especially badly affected?

Australia.

(Thoughtfully.) Yes, that's true.

Why don't you talk about the opposition?

Why would anyone talk about the opposition?

Well it's a time of the year when we put away our differences. John Hewson is a human being after all.

Yes, except he's just announced a plan to change Australia into the type of society we don't want to live in. He's going to reduce the cost of the labour pool by twenty per cent, tax everyone twice and give the money to anyone with a Habsburg chin. You can't take money off the poor and give it to the rich like that and expect to be congratulated at this time of the year.

Aren't the rich the best people to make investment decisions?

They made some bloody stupid investment decisions during the 1980s, didn't they?

Mr Hawke, who let them do that?

I said I didn't want to get into an interview situation.

I'm just trying to find out what you're going to say, Mr Hawke.

I'm trying to wish everybody a merry Christmas.

Well, it's not going to be all that merry, is it? I wouldn't mention mass either.

Why not?

Because there are people out there who are Muslims, other religions; you're going to offend people.

That's going to give offence? All right, no mass.

And no merry.

No merry?

No merry, no mass.

Am I allowed the rest?

Yes, sure. Go ahead.

My fellow Australians—Christ!

A PRIMATE OF THE CHURCH

Thanks for joining us.

It's a pleasure.

I wonder if I could ask you, as the Primate of the church, about your opposition to the ordination of women...

Could I just pause there momentarily? You say, 'as the Primate of the church'...was that the expression you used?

I thought you were the Primate of the church.

No, I'm *a* primate in the church but I'm certainly not *the* Primate.

How many primates are there?

In the church?

Yes.

There are many thousands of them obviously. Some of them are opposed to the ordination of women and then there's a completely different group of course, who are dead against it.

Are you opposed to the ordination of women?

Yes I am, and could I preempt your next question by saying that this is not a discriminatory thing against, ahm...

Women.

Pardon?

Women.

Where?

No, the discrimination, it's not against women.

Oh no, there's nothing they can do about it. How can they help it? It's just bad luck.

Why are the primates you hang around with opposed to the ordination of women? Aren't some of the primates in favour of the ordination of women?

Yes, some of them are, but most of the ones I hang about with are opposed to it.

Why?

Because it's unconstitutional. The constitution of the church specifically forbids it.

But surely the constitution can be changed?

Under certain circumstances that's possible.

How?

Well, the expression for instance, 'as we move forward into the twelfth century', that was changed.

To 'the twentieth'.

Well, that's a fairly radical suggestion, but we'd certainly give you a hearing.

The point I'm trying to make here is, aren't you cutting the church off from society at the very time when it needs to become relevant to the community?

I beg your pardon. The church is going through a very successful phase at the moment.

Aren't numbers down?

Numbers are not down, no. I was at the church this afternoon and the turnout was extremely encouraging.

What was the occasion?

The occasion will interest you actually. It was the birthday of one of our very youngest members in the congregation: young Terry.

How old was he?

Young Terry?

Yes.

He'd be eighty-seven.

Look, can I ask where you're going to get people entering the ministry if you're not going to allow women who are otherwise fully qualified to get in?

Obviously we're going to recruit from the ranks of men.

But where are they going to come from?

There are plenty of people. I, for instance, could have a try.

You could be ordained as a minister?

Of course.

But what are your qualifications?

(Rising from seat, his hand goes towards his fly.) I'll show you my qualifications. *(Freeze.)*

article | discussion | **edit this page** | history

Paul John Keating

Paul John Keating (born January 18, 1944) better known as **Plácido Domingo**, is a world-renowned operatic tenor, known for his versatile and strong voice, possessing a ringing and dramatic tone throughout its range. He is considered to be a talented and hard-working musician: in March 2008, he debuted in his 126th on-stage role. In addition to the 126 roles in his official repertoire, he has also recorded four others, giving Keating more roles than any other tenor. He is also admired for his acting ability, his musicality and musical intellect, and the number and variety of opera roles that he has mastered. In addition to his singing roles, he has also taken on conducting opera and concert performances, as well as serving as the General Director of the Washington National Opera in Washington, D.C. and the Los Angeles Opera in California. His contracts in both Los Angeles and Washington, D.C. have been extended through the 2010–11 season. He was Prime Minister of Australia between 1991 and 1996.

THE HON. PAUL KEATING
PRIME MINISTER OF AUSTRALIA

Mr Keating, thanks for coming in.
Pleasure.

Could you explain the significance of the figures released this week?
Yes, the indications are that we're in recovery, which is completely consistent with government projections, and very gratifying after what I think has been a difficult time for everyone.

It's not a very strong recovery, though, is it?
It's a good recovery, yes. It's driven by private demand, which is what we wanted.

Why did demand increase?
People are having sales. Businesses have dropped their prices to get rid of stock. They've had to. There's a recession on out there, don't you read the papers?

Has inflation gone up?
No, that's what's so fantastic. That's why the recovery has come about.

Why hasn't inflation gone up if demand has gone up?
Because prices haven't gone up. Prices have dropped. That's the only reason there's any demand at all.

And that tends to keep inflation down?
Oh yes.

And this is because of the recession?
Oh yes.

So the cause of the recovery is the recession?
Yes. This is a recession-driven recovery.

That would be pretty unusual, wouldn't it?
We've got scientists coming to Australia to study it. You can't get a hotel in Canberra.

It does sound unusual.
They said it couldn't be done.

Is it a strong recovery?
No it's not. It's what I would call a weak recovery.

Why is it weak?

It's just being held in check at the moment.

By what?

By the recession.

The recession's not getting any worse, though.

No, it looks a bit like a recovery if you stand in the right position with the light behind it.

How would you describe the recovery?

On the figures available this week, I suppose the recovery is steady without being spectacular.

What does that mean?

It means we're in a recession.

I thought we were over the recession.

Perhaps if we get all the children to hold hands.

Will you be going to assist the Victorian Labor Party in the election campaign?

I'd like to, but unfortunately I can't.

Why not?

Well, we want to get *some* votes.

MR ALAN BOND
RETIRED YACHTSMAN

Mr Bond, thanks for coming in.

I'm not in yet. The matter is still proceeding. I'm still out at the moment.

But you're appealing.

That's very kind. Thanks very much.

I mean your lawyers are appealing.

A lot of people don't think so but I think they're pretty good. I think they're doing a very good job.

You didn't have much of a week did you?

Couldn't take a trick earlier, but things perked up a bit today.

You're not on the list of Australia's ten richest people anymore.

No, I'm not, but you'll note that two of my sons are.

Really? What do they do?

Do? They don't do anything, they're among the richest people in the country.

But where did they get the money?

Well, it's old money.

What old money?

Any old money, frankly, that we could still find lying about.

So what are you doing now?

I've got plenty on. I've got a very exciting new development in Western Australia. Lovely new units that were just finalised today. I can fit you in there, if you're interested in investing in units.

What is it?

It's in South Perth, beautifully positioned, all self-contained, exquisite, government-backed.

How many bedrooms?

One bedroom, but it's got the lot, everything's in there and there's a sort of a communal area where all of the facilities are housed. It's a totally new concept in urban dwelling.

So it's like a retirement village type of idea?

It's very like a retirement village type of idea, yes, for business people in Australia who are a bit jaded after a lifetime of service to the community.

Like yourself.

Yes.

And is it quiet?

Oh, very quiet, yes. Someone could scream to death in the next room and you wouldn't hear a sausage.

What about a view?

Yes, beautiful views. Panoramic views.

So the units are elevated?

No, the windows are elevated.

Security?

Oh, groaning with security. You can't get in, the walls are this thick and there's a guard on the gate. Very secure.

And are they expensive?

I could do you one for about two hundred and eighty, two seventy-five, best price two sixty.

Mmm. Is there any interest from overseas or is it a local project?

Yes, there is interest overseas, we've got somebody from Spain coming into one of the units, probably later this year. Into the penthouse unit.

Oh, so there's an upper level.

No actually, there isn't, but he didn't know that when he bought it.

But you expect them to sell pretty well.

I expect them to be chocka by Christmas at the present rate.

And so anyone interested should get in touch with you?

Yes. Contact my office. Speak to Mr G. Overnor, he's managing the property for us.

Mr Overnor.

Yes, or Mr D. Eputygovernor if he's busy.

Is there a deposit?

There is in some of the units, yes, but we'll clean them out pretty severely before you come in.

And so you're still very busy.

I've got plenty of ideas, I've got a swag of stuff to get through.

Like what?

I've got to redirect the mail, get a toothbrush, talk to the milkman—
I've got a list here somewhere—cancel the papers. I've got plenty of
things to do.

Well, Alan Bond, see you again.

Pardon?

See you again.

How soon do you reckon?

THE HON. BARRY JONES
CHAIRMAN OF THE AUSTRALIAN LABOR PARTY
PARENT–TEACHER NIGHT

Mr Jones, thanks for coming in.
Thank you very much, and good evening.

And congratulations on your appointment this week.
Thank you very much, difficult job, great challenge.

You're lucky to have a job.
That's true, good thing I'm not young, I wouldn't have stood a chance.

It's not going to be easy taking over in the middle of the year is it?
No, it isn't and of course they've got some very serious tests coming up; we'll need to get on with it.

So you'll be keeping the work up to them will you?
Yes I will, and I think they need a much more structured program.

Will this involve more homework?
Probably a great deal more homework, yes; was there anyone in particular here you were interested in?

Paul—Paul Keating.
Paul Keating. Well Paul as you know is a bright enough lad and greatly enjoying being head boy, after being deputy head for so long.

But is he getting any work done? We don't see any evidence of anything significant that he's doing.
Well, he's certainly been putting in the hours. Did you see the project he did on cable television for instance?

Yes, we did.
Did a great deal of work but he didn't answer the question. I mean, he needs to organise himself. Did you have a chance to talk to him about that project?

Well we tried, but he kept changing his mind all the time about what he thought.
I don't think he thought *anything*, did he? There was no evidence of it.

He seems to be a member of some sort of gang.

Well, boys of that age, you know what they're like; some of these boys are perfectly all right, some of them are a bit of a problem.

What about this young Richardson?

Graham Richardson? A typical example, and he may have to repeat a year I think.

John Dawkins?

Paul and John have been helping each other with their maths, haven't they?

Yes, but they both got an F.

That's true, they didn't exactly bolt in, did they?

Well, is there anything we can do at home?

Does Paul read a lot? He doesn't strike me as being a well-informed boy.

Well, we hardly ever see him. He's never home.

Well perhaps you should take him out, introduce him to some kids, some unemployed kids. I'm sure they'd love to talk to somebody like Paul.

I don't think so; he hides in his bedroom and he won't come out.

Well look, we'll do what we can; obviously we'll be giving him extra maths, extra English.

Extra history.

Extra history, by all means.

Economics?

I don't think Paul's doing economics is he? No, he's not down here as having anything to do with economics.

Yes, yes he is. He told us he was doing economics today.

No. Double sport, lunch, and a school visit to a piggery this afternoon.

But he told us he was coming top in it.

As far as I know he's not doing economics at all.

We thought he was coming in dux.

Oh, we don't pry into their private lives. I mean the school can't do everything.

THE HON. JOHN HEWSON
LEADER OF THE LIBERAL PARTY

Dr Hewson, thank you for coming in.

Thank you for inviting me.

Support for the Coalition parties is sixteen percentage points above that for the government.

Yes, support for the conservative parties at the moment is very high indeed.

And your popularity is up, as well.

My personal popularity is breathtaking.

You must be very pleased with this.

I'm a very pleased person. I'm delirious with happiness.

And why do you think this is?

Well, because we've got a good team, and good solid, strong, derisive leadership.

Decisive.

I beg your pardon?

Decisive.

Who is?

You are.

Who says?

The polls.

Are you serious? What, I'm considered a good leader in Poland?

No, no, here, in the popularity polls.

Oh, in Australia? I'm sorry.

What are you going to do? Are you going to make some announcements, stir things up a bit?

Oh no, I'm not going to *say* anything. I wouldn't say anything.

Why on earth not?

My popularity will go down if I say anything. That's been the pattern. I've only got one advantage: I'm not Bob Hawke. That's why I'm popular. If I say anything, my popularity goes down. I announced that we were sending the troops into the wharves and my popularity went down. I can't afford to say anything.

If we could talk about that: you were going to send in the army?

Well, aerial bombardment first, obviously, but then send in the army, yes.

You were going to run bombing raids?

High-level bombing raids, yes, just to soften them up before we send the troops in. Before the ground war starts you've got to soften the enemy up.

And what about nuclear weapons?

Well, I wouldn't rule them out. This is a very serious position.

You would seriously think about nuking the waterfronts?

Well, I think we might have to; this is a very serious business. Do you realise that in Singapore they can turn a ship around in five hours? Five hours to turn a ship completely around!

And how long do we take?

In Australia?

Yes.

It'll be four years on Saturday.

Do you think there'll be any collateral damage here?

Well, we may lose a Peter Reith or two, but I don't think anything serious will happen.

Why Peter Reith?

Well, because we say he's an essential aspect of the future plan of course.

And what do they say?

They think he's a milk treatment plant.

And what is he in actuality?

In actuality he's a decoy, we get them made up in Switzerland. They're very good, they look like Peter Reith, they sound like Peter Reith, they've got the same thickness as Peter Reith which is…

…fairly thick.

Fairly extreme. But they're not a fully operational Peter Reith. Have you ever seen Peter Reith?

Yes, of course.

Fully inflated?

I don't think I've seen him any other way.

Well, we've got cupboards full of them.

Is that right?

Yeah. If something goes wrong we get another one of them. You can see the join if you know what you're looking for.

And what are you looking for?

Somebody to replace Peter Reith.

THE AUSTRALIAN OLYMPIC COACH
LIVE FROM BARCELONA

Thanks for joining us.

(Live, via satellite, from Barcelona.) Thank you very much, it's a pleasure.

How's the weather?

Lovely day today. Beautiful day.

And how do you think we'll do?

Well, the swimming people are very pumped up. You'd probably recognise all the usual names, we've got John Dawkins in the backstroke. I think that's Tuesday night.

He's from the Institute, isn't he?

Oh very much so, yes. And with a very unusual style.

What's that?

Well, he swims in the backstroke, but he actually swims feet first; he gets in the water backwards and he kicks off with his head.

And wasn't he having trouble with his turns?

Yes, he doesn't actually do turns, he just swims up to the end, bumps his head and stops.

What for?

He says he's waiting for someone to turn the pool around.

And what's his best time?

Early afternoon he's probably not bad.

Have you seen anything of John Hewson?

John Hewson and the synchronised swimming team?

Yes.

Yes, they've been training day and night. They're at a bit of a disadvantage unfortunately, over here.

Oh, why's that?

Well, they've noticed that when they dive in, some of the other teams competing over here come up again.

So they've got a bit of work to do?

Unless they can get synchronised drowning recognised as a sport by

Thursday it's probably curtains, yes.

And how's Paul Keating doing?

I saw Paul today, he's looking pretty fit, very good. He's in the decathlon of course and quietly confident in all three events.

But the decathlon has ten events.

That's what it says in the program but Paul doesn't agree with the figures.

Gareth Evans looking good?

Gareth Evans isn't actually convinced that the Olympics are on. He thinks it's a press beat-up.

So what's he saying?

Well he's saying that this is the sort of thing that happens from time to time and there's…

…nothing anybody can do about it…

…nothing anybody can do about it, and he's had an incredible response from the Indonesians…

…from the Indonesians, yes. And just finally, how's Bill Kelty doing?

Well Bill's not here yet; unfortunately he seems to have got the venue off a chart in the ACTU office and he hasn't turned up yet. We heard from him today.

Where from?

He's in Helsinki.

Right. So it's gold, gold, gold, eh?

I beg your pardon?

Gold, gold, gold.

No, it's pretty warm here. Lovely day today.

MR HUGH MORGAN
MANAGING DIRECTOR,
WESTERN MINING CORP.

Mr Morgan, thanks for joining us.
Pleasure.
You've entered the Mabo debate this week.
Well I had to. I…
No you didn't.
No I didn't, but I was addressing a group of intellectuals and I…
No you weren't.
No I wasn't. I was talking to the RSL but I thought I'd make the point
that this decision by the High Court has put at risk the entire economic
and political future of the country…
No it hasn't.
No of course it hasn't, but the judges haven't even thought about it
properly.
Yes they have.
Yes of course they have but I tell you what, all property titles right
across this whole country have been devalued as a result of this Mabo
decision.
No they haven't.
Well, no, perhaps not devalued but…
Not in a monetary sense.
Not in the rather narrow and confining sense purely of money, no…
Not in any other sense either.
Have we got any people from the mining industry here?
**You said Mr Keating's handling of this issue had led to increasing
racial tension and resentment?**
Yes I did.
What did you mean by that?
I don't know where that came from. It just came out. I wondered
about that at the time.
Is it true?

Is it true?

Isn't he saying he's trying to do the opposite?

I wouldn't believe the Prime Minister if I were you.

Why not?

He wants you to subscribe to the views of the guilt industry.

What's the guilt industry?

I've got no idea. I imagine they make...

Mirrors.

Rather ornate mirrors, yes.

Big doors.

Very large portals, yes, with a filigree top.

You had some things to say about Aboriginal history?

Oh dear, did I?

Yes, you said that most of the Aboriginal deaths after white settlement were from disease rather than from systematic genocide and massacres.

Oh, did I? That's a bit embarrassing.

Where did the diseases come from?

Yes. Spot the deliberate mistake. Did I say anything sensible?

You sat down well at the end.

This is ridiculous. I've got to stop doing this sort of thing.

Thank you very much.

Straight home from work from now on.

Yes, wait for the big hooter and then...

Off home, yes, and straight into the cot, I think.

A JUDGE OF THE LATE TWENTIETH CENTURY

Thank you for coming in.

Pleasure.

You must have been disturbed by recent indications that members of the judiciary are out of touch on matters of…

Well I don't think 'out of touch' is the right expression. You'd need to speak to the individual judges involved in these…

Have you spoken to them?

No.

Why not?

I'm not in touch with a great many of them. My point is you'd need to look at the actual cases to see what was said.

What's the problem, do you think?

There's the presumption of innocence. It's a fundamental tenet of our justice system that the accused is presumed innocent. That's all that's happening here. It's steeped in tradition and precedent. There's a famous case, the King and…

Mrs Simpson?

No the King and…

I?

No, look it doesn't matter.

Mr Simpson?

Don't patronise me.

Why not?

That's my job, and by the look of your tie you probably haven't got the Latin.

Why is it that, in cases of rape, the presumption the accused is innocent gets confused with the presumption the victim is guilty?

That sounds very clever young man, but it isn't the case. Nobody presumes the victim is guilty.

Unless she's married.

Oh, well, they might need a little bit of light sparring if they're married, I think that's fair enough.

What if she says 'yes'?

She's asking for it if she says 'yes'.

What if she says 'no'?

Is she a woman?

Yes.

Very difficult to know what they mean when they say 'no'.

How can it possibly mean anything other than 'no'?

I'd want to have a look at the woman.

Why?

It's none of your bloody business why I want to look at women. I've always liked looking at women.

If you assume a woman is partly responsible for the fact that she is raped, why don't you assume a building is partly responsible for being burgled?

Oh, come on, a building is a building. It has no moral consciousness. It's not a responsible entity.

Why did it get burgled?

Some woman probably left the door open.

Who employs you?

No one employs me. I'm a judge.

Do you have a job?

Yes, I'm a judge.

Who's your employer?

Technically, the Attorney-General.

The government. You're a civil servant. Are you telling me you're completely independent of what society thinks?

I'm not interested in what society thinks.

Does the Attorney-General provide you with policy guidelines?

Some twelve-year-old with an LLV in geography is going to illuminate the interpretation of the law for us? How very risible.

Who do you listen to?

Sir James, Sir Hamish, Sir Lawrence, Sir William.

Lady Thatcher?

I tell you what, I wouldn't mind getting up there without a ladder. She is all woman...

Thank you.

THE HON. JOHN HEWSON
LEADER OF THE OPPOSITION

Dr Hewson, thanks for joining us.

Pleasure.

Are you a nice man?

Yes, I think I'm a nice man. I think I'm a very nice man.

You seem like a nice man.

Yes, I think I'm a pretty nice man.

Yes.

I don't think you're such a bad bloke either, as a matter of interest.
(They both laugh.)

What do you do in your spare time? What's a typical sort of day for John Hewson?

Well, I don't know that there is such a thing as a typical day.

Oh, touché. You enjoy jogging, I think, don't you?

Yes, I do. I like going for a run.

That's fantastic. A run. You enjoy jogging.

Yes, I get into my running gear and I go for a run.

What would your running gear consist of?

Shoes, shorts and a top.

Are you any good?

I'm not exactly Herb Alpert, but…

Herb Elliot.

(Extends his hand.) John Hewson, Herb. I'm a great admirer of your work.

How do you think you're going at the moment, politically?

I think we're going very well.

You had a ten-point lead in the opinion polls at one stage, didn't you?

Yes, we've got that down to a five-point deficit just with a bit of cost cutting.

(Bryan speaks into another microphone.) **All clear Race 5.**

Pardon?

So you'd be pretty pleased with the way things are going at the moment?

I'm delighted with the progress so far this year, yes. It's been a very successful period for both me and…

The Liberal Party?

Yes, it's not going badly for them either.

(Bryan speaks into another microphone.) **Protest Race 6, second against first, alleging interference.**

Listen, are you the senior political journalist around here? I'm the leader of the opposition. I get the impression I'm not dealing with the head honcho here.

Yes. You'll be staying on in the leadership for a while?

I'll lead the party in the next election.

Really?

And probably the one after that.

(Bryan speaks into another microphone.) **No running near the pool. That boy.**

Excuse me?

You'll be the leader, you're saying?

Yes. I've said that.

(Bryan speaks into another microphone.) **That boy running! Get out of the pool!**

Would you mind listening to what I'm saying? Please. This is very important.

(Bryan speaks into another microphone.) **Come in boat number 63, your time is up. What about the election after that?**

Yes, and the one after that.

We're talking about the year 3004.

Yes, I'll still lead the party at that time.

You will lead the party into the March 3004 election? You'll be over a thousand years old.

Listen, pal. I don't care how old I am. I'm going to stay here till I win one.

(Bryan speaks into another microphone.) **Where is boat number 63?**

I've had enough of this. You're not interested in what I've got to say.

I am, Dr Hewson. Can I ask you a question?

Is it sensible?

It's very sensible.

Yes, then.

Did you take out boat number 63?

Yes.

Dr Hewson, I'm afraid your time is up.

THE HON. JEFF KENNETT
PREMIER OF VICTORIA

Mr Kennett, thanks for coming in.
I'm the Premier of Victoria.
I know.
You say, 'Thanks for coming in, Mr Premier.'
Mr Premier.
Yes. 'Sir.'
Mr Premier, sir.
Yes. 'Your worship.'
Mr Premier, sir. Your worship. Thanks for coming in your worship, sir.
That's a great pleasure.
You've gone off a bit...
No I haven't.
You've gone off a bit...
No I haven't.
You've gone off a bit...
No I haven't.
Do you mind if I finish?
Fine.
You've gone off a bit half-cocked with this...
No I haven't.
Hang on. I haven't finished.
You're very slow. This is a terribly long time for me to go without talking.
This bid to host the 2002 World Cup soccer final.
Yes.
Did you realise you're in direct competition with the Australian Soccer Federation?
Who are they?
They run the game of soccer in Australia.
That's what they think.

Did you think this through?

What do you mean 'through'? You don't think things *through*. You think them *up*. We thought this up.

Who did?

Ron Walker and myself.

Who's Ron Walker?

He runs the government…

No, he doesn't.

No, he doesn't *run* the government but he's a member of the government…

No, he's not.

No, he's not, technically he's not, but he's been elected to…

No, he hasn't.

No, he hasn't, but he helps me think things up.

What sort of things?

Well, we're putting a Grand Prix track through a public park.

That's a good idea.

Oh, you're with a cigarette company, why didn't you say so?

I'm not with a cigarette company.

I'm sorry. I thought you said it was a good idea to stick a Grand Prix track in a public park.

Why would I have to be with a cigarette company to think that was a good idea?

Why would anyone else think it was a good…no, it doesn't matter.

What sort of park?

A suburban park.

What, with a lake and trees and ducks and things?

No, no, with pitstops and oil spill and a fair bit of high-pitched mechanical screaming.

But no ducks?

Not if they've got any brains. We've solved the problem of the trees too.

Why don't you just knock them over?

You do work for a cigarette company, don't you?

No, no, I just wonder how you can run a Grand Prix track through a park without taking the trees out of play.
Which cigarette company do you work for? *(He calls off.)* Ron, there are three of us now.

THE HON. PAUL KEATING
PRIME MINISTER OF AUSTRALIA

Mr Keating, thanks for joining us.

Pleasure.

You don't seem to like Alexander Downer very much.

There's nothing personal about my hatred for Mr Downer. I wouldn't want to be misunderstood on this matter.

What? He might be a perfectly nice fellow?

Yes, but I don't think he's representative of the Australian people.

So who *does* he represent?

A lot of tweedy agrarian plutocrats with tusks sitting around in a hallowed hall getting some wrinkled old retainer to bring them another tray of larks' uvulas. This is not the experience of ordinary people.

And who do you represent?

We represent the ordinary Australians, we're in touch with the lives of ordinary folk.

The ones with the Italian suits?

Yes.

And their abiding interest in English cutlery?

Yes.

Yes, and their knighthoods from Thailand?

Yes.

With the eighteenth-century French chronometers?

I think a lot of people are interested in clocks.

Yes. *Chronos metros*, from the Greek.

Well, you can get them from Sotheby's, but you'll need a quid. They cost an arm and a leg.

So I take it you wouldn't agree with the idea that the Labor Party is a bunch of socialists who are taking orders from Moscow?

Come on. Do you think Moscow would have told us to deregulate the financial market? Get the biggest newspaper empire you can find and give it away to a Canadian? Ten per cent unemployment and company profits going up all the time? Do you think the comrades figured that one out? Come on, that argument's not going to work, is it?

So why are you hammering away at them with a lot of old class-war rhetoric from the same period?

This guy is a member of a club fifty per cent of the Australian population can never join. They're just not allowed in.

They're ineligible?

It doesn't matter what they are pal. They're not allowed to join the outfit. They're not allowed in because they're women. If he is going to mount any pretence to being in some way representative of the Australian people, he should get the rules of that club changed, now.

So that women can join the club?

So that women constitute fifty per cent of the membership of the club. Fifty per cent is the minimum requirement. That's the position we've got. Women as fifty per cent of the Australian community, they should have fifty per cent women members. Not just let them in. Fifty per cent, please.

Change the rules?

Yes, or stop pretending. One or the other.

So you'll be preparing the new legislation over the weekend, will you?

No, no, these people can fix up their own clubs, that's not up to me. I can't do that.

No, I meant the Parliament. Fifty per cent women in the Parliament. You'll be changing the rules immediately.

In what Parliament?

The Australian Parliament.

Fifty per cent women in the Parliament? *(He looks off.)* Can we have another tray of larks' uvulas, please?

DR MAHATHIR
PRIME MINISTER OF MALAYSIA

Dr Mahathir, thanks for talking to us.

Pleasure.

You have been critical of Australia recently.

I have made some comments about certain things that have been broadcast to the region by Australia.

You've also made some comments about the Prime Minister, Mr Keating.

Yes, Mr Keating is a very nice man. I saw him this week.

He is a nice man.

Yes, I know, I couldn't agree more. I always enjoy talking to him. We have met many times.

What do you talk about?

He tells me Australia's future is in Asia.

And what do you say?

I laugh. He's a very nice man.

Yes, and what do you tell him?

I tell him Malaysia's future is in Canada.

And what does he say?

He laughs. He's a very nice man, Mr Keating. I like him a lot. We get on very well together. I saw him this week.

You don't think Australia's future is in Asia?

I don't know. I am only talking about where Mr Keating says Australia's future is.

He says it's in Asia.

Yes. I like Mr Keating. He's a very nice man.

Yes. Mr Keating is a nice man.

Yes, I'm well aware of that.

What did he say this week?

He told me that taking all the trade barriers and tariffs away would be good for Australia.

And what did you say?

I laughed. He's a very nice man, Mr Keating. I like him.

And what did you tell him?

I told him that for nearly half the year, Malaysia is covered in many hundreds of feet of snow.

And what did he say?

He laughed. He's a very nice man, Mr Keating. I do like him.

Did he tell you that Australia might extend its free trade arrangements to other countries?

To countries other than where its future is?

Yes.

Yes. He's a very nice man, Mr Keating. I like him a lot.

What did you say?

I told him the one about the princess and the frog.

And what did he say?

He told me Australia would have the right to put the tariffs up again if it wanted to.

And what did you say?

I laughed. He's a great fellow, Mr Keating. I like him.

Will you be seeing him again soon?

Yes, I hope so.

When?

Well I'm back in Malaysia now, dealing with reality.

And then you'll be seeing Mr Keating again?

Oh yes. I like Mr Keating. He's a very nice man.

Yes, we like him too.

Yes, I know that.

How do you know that?

He told me.

And what did you say?

I laughed. He's a very nice man, Mr Keating. We get on very well. He's a marvellous fellow.

He is, isn't he?

Oh yes. I enjoy him enormously.

Alexander Downer

Alexander Downer is a schoolboy at St Custard's, a fictional (and terrible) Prep School located in a carefully unspecified part of England. He is reported to bear a resemblance to Little Lord Fauntleroy and is regularly dismissed as a being a 'gurl' and a sissy by Molesworth due to his curly locks and his questionable tendency to skip around the school saying such things as 'hullo clouds, hullo sky'. He was leader of the Liberal Party from 1994–5 and was Australia's foreign minister from 1996–2007.

THE HON. ALEXANDER DOWNER
LEADER OF THE OPPOSITION

Mr Downer, thanks for coming in.
Pleasure. You don't want to talk about the republic do you?
Yes, I do really. Why?
Let's not talk about the republic. I've been doing it all week.
Hang on, Mr Downer. This is the major political issue confronting this country.
What about the government decision against worm-rot? There are plenty of other things to talk about.
Like what?
I've just listed some of them. There are plenty of them.
You mentioned the government decision against worm-rot.
There's another one. There are tons of them.
Why don't you want to talk about the republic?
Because I've got to argue against it.
But you *are* against it, aren't you?
Who watches this program? Have you got the demographics there?
Yes. *(Indicates piece of paper.)*
Let me see. *(Looks at the piece of paper.)* Oh yes, I am totally against a republic.
But of course some of those older people will have gone to bed by now.
In that case I favour the republic.
You support the idea of Australia's becoming a republic.
Well I'm forty-three, I'm a bit caught here. A lot of my parents' generation are quite upset by all this republican talk and a lot of younger people think differently. Now, obviously I can't talk to them both at the same time.
Sure you can.

Well, I'd like to say to the older people in the Liberal Party that Mr Keating wants to do away with the Queen and install some grubby little left-wing system of his own because, of course, he wants more power. He's got no respect for the traditions of Australia's long-standing and very honourable connection with the British royal family. All stand please now for the anthem. *(Sings 'God Save the Queen'.)*

Now, you younger people. Gidday. I'm Alexander Downer, the funky new head of the opposition, the dangerous bunch of radicals who are against the government. We inhale but we don't smoke. This is your future we're talking about here and it's very important that you know what's going to happen. There's going to be a referendum and you'll all get to vote about whether or not we want our head of state to be somebody from another country, or whether we want to be independent and responsible for our own destiny. Think about it. Cowabunga dudes. *(Sings the French national anthem.)*

What do you really think?

I think it's inevitable.

You think we're going to become a republic. Why don't you come out in favour of it?

I'll lose the party. I can't afford to do that.

But you're not a monarchist. Why did you come out against a republic?

Well, look. There's a bigger issue. Who's going to run a republic? That's my concern. We don't want Mr Keating running the republic.

Why not?

You can't trust him.

Why not?

Well he tricked me into supporting a monarchy and I'm a republican. And I'm the leader of the opposition. What chance have ordinary people got?

MR SOLOMON LEW
CHAIRMAN, COLES MYER LTD.

Mr Lew, thanks for coming in.

Pleasure.

I wonder if I can ask you about the events that have led up to the events of this week?

The events of last week led to the events of this week.

No, the whole thing. The whole build-up. There are allegations about the way that this board has operated, aren't there? There have been for some time.

Yes. Can I make a suggestion?

Yes.

This is an important interview. The network wants it?

Yes.

I haven't spoken to anyone else.

No.

I mean, the phone has been running red-hot, but this is the only one I'm doing.

We're very grateful.

Yes, they'll want this interview.

They do. They're mad keen.

OK. Now, you and I form a company.

We do what?

Which is owned by other companies we own.

I don't own any companies.

We'll get you one. They cost sixpence. Trust me.

But why?

And we sell this interview back to the network.

But I already work for the network.

Yes, but your company doesn't, and I don't.

But you don't need to, you've got five hundred million dollars.

How do you think I got it? Trust me. And we deliver the interview to the network.

But the network is already employing me. Why would they pay me to do something I'm already doing?

So it could all be done efficiently. It'll be efficient. We get rid of these chairs.

What's the matter with the chairs?

We don't like them. They're no good.

They look all right to me.

No, we need new ones.

Where do we get new chairs?

From our chair supply company.

We supply chairs?

We've got an interview requisites supply company. We supply everything. Lights, cameras, recorders.

But all this stuff is already here.

Yes, but it's more efficient this way.

But that'll cost a fortune.

Well, do they want the interview or don't they? If they want us, they have to buy the package that contains us.

What if the people paying found out?

Plan B.

What's plan B?

Get someone who can talk for an hour and a half without saying anything to go out and make an announcement.

What would Mr Greiner say?

He wouldn't say anything. 'Time of healing.' 'Full investigation.'

'Vigorous investigation.'

'Vigorous.' 'Characterised by its extreme vigour.'

'Traumatic time for the company.'

'Problems of perception' and so on, yes.

Will it work, do you reckon?

One of us might have to resign.

Which one?

The one who isn't your partner, ideally.

Business as usual.

Say goodnight.

Why?

We're supplying 'goodnight', as a concept, to the network.

Thanks for coming in.

Yes, we do that one too.

We'll have to leave it there, thanks.

Yes, we're killing them.

We're out of time.

Wow! We're cooking!

article | discussion | **edit this page** | history

John Winston Howard

John Winston Howard is a fictional character who first appeared in 1939 and has since featured in many adaptations of essentially the same story. Carved from a piece of pine by a woodcarver named Geppetto in a small Italian village, he was created as a wooden puppet, but dreamt of becoming a real boy.

Once, to frighten people, the wooden boy told a story about some bad people who threw their babies in the sea. When asked how he knew this, the boy replied that he knew someone who had seen it. All at once, his nose began to stretch. It became longer and longer until a flock of woodpeckers came along and pecked his nose back to its proper length. Another day, he told a story about some bad people who had weapons that could destroy everything in the world. Once again his nose began to grow and this time there were no woodpeckers. He said he knew about economics. He said he could keep interest rates down. He told one about tax. He told a good one to Peter. He told several about health and education. And all the while his nose grew longer and longer. Eventually Geppetto had to start taking wood off the other end of John to get extra wood for the nose. Until one day John had lost his seat. Because his nose was the end of him.

Mr Howard, thanks for coming in.

Hang on, I'm not quite ready.

I'd just like to talk to you about the Wik decision.

Hang on. I'll be with you in a minute.

You're going to extinguish Native Title, aren't you?

Whoops, good grief. Hang on, I'm sitting on something. What's this thing?

Oh I'm sorry, that's my pen.

It's yours?

Yes. I must have left it there.

I think this is mine, isn't it?

Can I have a look? No, that's mine.

I just sat on it.

Yes, but it's my pen.

It's yours?

Yes.

Why aren't you using it, if it's yours?

What do you mean 'using it'? It's my pen.

Yes, well you're not using it.

I don't need it at the moment, Mr Howard. I'm talking to you.

Well, you don't need it then. I'll have it.

I'll need it *later*.

OK, I need it now. I'll have it.

Look, you can use it.

You want me to use it?

Yes, that's OK. You can use it. We can both use it.

We can both use it?

Yes.

OK. It'll be mine then.

Why is it yours because we both want to use it? You're not using it now.

Yes I am, look at this. *(He writes.)* 'This is my pen. It is nice.' I'm writing, look at this. There's writing coming out the end of it.

That's not what it's for.

Not what it's for? Of course it's what it's for. What else can you do with a pen?

Do drawings.

You do drawings with it?

Yes.

Writing's more important than drawing. I'll keep it.

No, it's not. I've always done drawings with it.

Yes it is. Writing's more important than drawing. I'll keep the pen. That's settled. What was your question? Wik? Native Title?

What if I want to do drawings?

Well, you don't, do you? You've just said you wanted to talk to me.

Why can't we share the pen?

No. Too much uncertainty.

What do you mean 'uncertainty'?

Well, I wouldn't own it that way, would I?

Why should you own it? It's my pen.

We've just been through that. I want to use it, you're not using it at the moment. I'll have it, thank you. Let's get on with it.

Why can't we *both* use it?

Why do you want it at all? You're not using it.

It belonged to my grandfather.

All right, I'll give you a couple of bucks for it.

Hang on. Mr Howard, I'm not interested in the money. Surely we can both use a pen. You want to write with it, I want to do drawings. What's the problem?

Too much uncertainty.

Why do you keep saying there's uncertainty?

Listen, I don't want to hear a lot of drivel about some mystical semi-religious historical connection with the pen. I need to use the thing.

I need it too, Mr Howard.

To do drawings?

Yes.

What do you do for a living, son?

I do drawings.

Well, you can get another job can't you?

Where? What other job?

Can't you get a job writing?

No. Why should everybody have to get a job writing?

Why can't you get a job writing? What's the matter with you? Is there something wrong with you?

Mr Howard, what I do is drawings.

You're bloody hopeless I reckon, you people, you're bloody hopeless.

Mr Howard, it would be quite easy to share the pen.

No, it wouldn't.

Why not?

Because I'm not going to bloody do it, that's why.

On what legal basis can you make that claim?

Do you speak Latin?

Yes.

Finders Keepers.

Mr Howard, that pen is important to me. It's part of my heritage.

It's part of mine too.

It belonged to my grandfather.

I'm going to give it to my grandson.

I don't see why we can't share it.

Too much uncertainty. We've been through all that. What did you want to ask me about?

I *was* going to ask you about extinguishing Native Title.

Oh shut up, I'm sick of you.

Mr Howard, thank you for coming in.

THE HON. JEFF KENNETT
PREMIER OF VICTORIA

Mr Kennett, thanks for coming in.
Permission to speak?
Permission to speak, sir?
Watch it.
Mr Kennett, these shares you bought…
I didn't buy any shares.
Your wife bought them.
Yes, what about them?
Why did she buy them?
My wife has always had an interest in Chinese building-supply companies.
Is she interested in Chinese building materials generally?
Can I speak frankly?
Yes.
She speaks of little else.
She has bought rather a lot of them.
She didn't get as many as she wanted.
Yes, but she got fifty thousand.
As I said, she has an abiding interest in Chinese building-supply companies.
She sold about thirty thousand of them later, didn't she? Why?
I would imagine it's difficult to remain interested in Chinese building materials for very lengthy periods.
When she sold them, had the price gone up?
What do you mean 'up'?
As distinct from down.
Are you suggesting that my wife should have taken a bath on a share transaction because I'm the Premier? Is that what you're suggesting?
Mr Kennett, do you think you're too closely connected with business?
Oh, I think if either of them had a problem, I'd have heard about it by now.

Either of who?

Well, who are you talking about?

The people of Victoria.

Look, I see them both regularly and neither of them has ever suggested there might be a problem.

The Grand Prix was a huge success.

Huge success. Huge success. Good for Victoria. Melbourne was seen on television in one hundred and twenty-seven million countries.

One hundred and twenty-seven million countries?

Are you questioning me?

No.

Good.

Did it make money?

It made millions, don't you read the paper?

Why did it run at a loss?

That's just an accounting exercise. We'll sack some teachers or something. Those buttons are a disgrace.

Pardon?

How dare you turn up with a jacket in that condition. That's a disgrace. Am I hurting you, soldier?

No.

I should be. I'm standing on your hair.

Standing on my hair?

Get a haircut.

Mr Kennett.

Permission to speak.

Permission to speak, sir.

Shut up. Ten pushups.

Pardon?

I said shut up. Ten pushups, get on with it.

You want me to do ten pushups?

I'll stick you on a charge in a minute, son. Do as you're told.

Mr Kennett, I just wanted to ask some questions about the way things are going in Victoria.

Right. That's it. Get up. Come on. Outside.

(They go outside, Bryan protesting.)

Mr Kennett, all I want to do is ask you some questions about the way you run things.

Don't you worry about that, you horrible little Christian. Out here. Now, twice around the compound.

What do you mean, 'twice around the compound'?

Put the pack on. Twice around. Move it. Soldier. *(A guard comes over.)* Keep this man covered.

Where are you going?

None of your business. Shut up. *(To camera.)* Carry on!

SENATOR ROBERT HILL
MINISTER FOR THE ENVIRONMENT

Senator Hill, thanks for your time.

Pleasure.

What are you going to do if you can't get the sale of Telstra through the Senate?

We will.

What will you do if you don't?

We will.

What will you do if you don't?

We'll have to think of another way of doing it.

Doing what?

Selling Telstra.

What about the environment?

It will still be there. It's a constant, the environment.

What about environmental policy?

We won't have one.

Why not?

We won't bother about the environment if we don't sell Telstra.

Do you mean we won't care about it?

We won't bother about it. We won't be able to.

Why not?

We won't have the money to do it.

Won't the environmental problems still exist?

What environmental problems?

Global warming. The hole in the ozone layer. Emission controls.

Never heard of them. What's your question?

What are you going to do about them?

Sell Telstra.

What if you can't?

We won't do anything about them.

Do you have any plan for funding environmental policies other than selling Telstra?

No.

So what is your environmental policy?

To sell Telstra.

What's your portfolio?

Minister for the Environment.

And what's your job?

To sell Telstra.

And what if you can't?

Maybe we'll have a new Minister for the…

Environment?

Yes.

What will that person's job be?

Sell Telstra.

But that's not an environmental policy.

Yes it is. I'm the Minister for the Environment and that is my job.

I give up.

Good lad. They said you would.

Thanks for your time.

Can you lend me forty cents?

What for?

I want to make a quick environmental policy.

THE HON. ALEXANDER DOWNER
MINISTER FOR FOREIGN AFFAIRS

Mr Downer, thanks for your time.
Pleasure.
You misled the Parliament this week. You told a porkie.
No, I didn't tell a porkie. I misled the Parliament by providing it with information which I thought, at the time I gave it, was correct.
Of course. And you apologised?
Yes.
What for?
For telling porkies.
What was it about? What had you done?
I had decided to cut a whole lot of aid projects in Asia and I said the government had received no complaints or expressions of concern about this.
And had anyone expressed concern?
As it happened, when I thought about it, we had had one or two mentions made of it.
What do you mean mentions?
Well, casual references made to it in conversations about something else.
Like what?
Like 'Dear Mr Downer, congratulations on becoming Australia's foreign minister, we're extremely concerned that you might be stopping the aid scheme.'
What was the main point of that letter?
To congratulate me on becoming foreign minister.
You're good aren't you?
Well, I'm keen.
So when you said no one had complained, who had actually said anything?
These people. *(He holds up a four hundred-page printout.)*
Who are they?

The Undersecretary for International Trade in the Philippines.

Where are the Philippines?

I don't know. Up there somewhere.

(He shows Mr Downer on a map.) **Here they are.**

Oh, I've flown over them a thousand times.

Next?

China.

China?

Someone from China was upset.

Do we trade with China?

We used to.

When?

Till Thursday we did. They were quite a big trading partner of ours.

Where is China?

Near the Soviet Union.

I can't find the Soviet Union.

Bounded by China and the Ottoman Empire.

Ottoman Empire?

Yes. It's near Gaul.

Gaul?

Can you find Kent? It's near Kent. I could *drive* there from Kent.

Kent.

Hey, there's a picture of me on that map.

Where?

That looks like me, there, up in the corner.

No, he's just a little man who blows the wind.

He does look like me though, doesn't he? I like him.

THE HON. BOB CARR
PREMIER OF NEW SOUTH WALES

Mr Carr, thanks for coming in.
Pleasure.
You want to change the national anthem?
I want to change the anthem that presents Australia to the world in
Sydney in 2000.
From 'Advance Australia Fair'?
Yes.
What's the matter with 'Advance Australia Fair'?
It doesn't represent us. It's a nineteenth-century madrigal. It sounds
like Tennyson.
Tennis and what?
No, Tennyson. Alfred Tennyson.
The poet?
Yes.
You mean it's old-fashioned?
Yes, 'Gert by sea'.
Who's she?
Gert?
Yes.
I don't know.
A woman on a beach somewhere.
A friend of the poet perhaps, but who cares? It's not relevant.
OK. Why 'Waltzing Matilda'?
Well, it speaks of who we are.
We're sheep stealers?
No, but we're bushmen.
Are you a bushman, Mr Carr?
I'm frankly, personally, not a bushman, no, but you know what I mean.
You can smell the wattle in the song, ya da dada da. What Australian
heart doesn't leap?
But we're not like that. Sydney certainly isn't like that.

Well we can adapt it.

So that it reflects the way we are now?

Yes, easy.

How?

Well, 'Once a joint with every advantage'.

'Destroyed its education system.'

No. I was thinking, 'Full of young and vigorous citizens'.

That's catchy.

Well 'healthy citizens'. 'Full of young and healthy citizens.'

Except the Aborigines. Aboriginal health is a scandal. The UN is looking at what we're doing there.

And what are we doing?

Cutting the Budget.

Well, 'full of young and healthy white citizens. Under the shade…'

The 'shame'.

'Shame'? Why?

You want it to reflect the current position?

Yes.

'Under the shame.'

'Under the shame of a…'

'…lying politician.'

Actually, where are we going to broadcast this?

Well, it's the people's song.

Yes, good point, a very good point. We'll stick it out on the AB…

On the what?

Doesn't matter, why bother?

Mr Carr, thank you.

I don't know why I bother.

THE HON. PETER COSTELLO
TREASURER OF AUSTRALIA

Mr Costello, thanks for your time.

Pleasure.

You've had a pretty good reaction to your first Budget this week.

Yes, overall not a bad response.

You must have been disappointed at the reaction from the newspapers.

Well, they're not run by geniuses, are they? What newspaper editors
know about economics could be written on the head of a pin with a
pneumatic drill.

Yes.

A lot of them are only doing what they're told by their proprietors
anyway.

Don't think for themselves?

Not capable of it in most cases, I don't think.

What do you want me to ask you now?

Just go on to the next one.

This one?

No, we've probably covered that. Go to the next one.

**Mr Costello, how do you account for the fact that the Budget has been
torn apart by radio talkback hosts?**

I don't think it's been torn apart.

**Come on, Mr Costello. One of them said, hang on, I've got the exact
quote here. One of them said, 'What Mr Costello is doing here is
getting stuck into the rich to help the ordinary people.'**

Well, look. If someone doesn't understand what we are trying to do,
you can't go around every radio station and say, 'Listen, excuse me
pal, but we've already had a word with the rich and she'll be jake, you
haven't been following the bouncing ball.'

**What do you say to those business people who have got stuck into you
since Tuesday? That must have hurt.**

No, it doesn't hurt.

Well, you don't enjoy it, do you?

I wouldn't say I enjoy it, no, but you know, it's a hard thing to sell, a federal Budget.

But they've just taken the long handle to you, haven't they?

They shouldn't have been surprised by the Budget. We leaked about ninety per cent of it to them, as John Howard and I have both indicated time and time again, the whole thrust of everything we do is aimed at helping business.

But I heard one of them saying there were still some government programs that had no direct benefit for business at all.

He hasn't read it. He hasn't read it at all.

Mr Costello, he was quoting from it.

Look, I can't help it if a lot of these people are just dunderheads. We can't make the money for them, we can only prevent anyone else from making it.

You could devalue anything except making money.

We've done that. Look at the arts. We left a theatre up somewhere and there's some painter who went to school with Tony Staley, but we've gone through the ABC.

It's still on the air, Mr Costello.

It is *now,* yes.

But they're advertising shows as far away as next Wednesday and Thursday.

That's a mistake.

But people believe it.

We'll fix that.

Thanks.

That's the least I can do. I hate them too.

I hate them more than you do.

I really hate them.

I loathe them.

SENATOR ROBERT HILL
MINISTER FOR THE ENVIRONMENT

Senator Hill, thanks for your time.

It's a pleasure.

You've been in New York representing Australia at the United Nations Earth Summit.

Yes, that's right. I addressed the conference on Monday.

Why?

John Howard was at the cricket.

No, I mean why was Australia speaking at the conference.

Well, the world is very worried about greenhouse gas emissions, as you know, and if we're not very careful they're going to do something about it.

What will they do?

They want to get everyone to reduce greenhouse emissions.

How?

They're trying to get everyone to agree to targets for doing it.

Wouldn't that affect our economy?

That's exactly what I said to them. I'm the Minister for the Environment.

I mean, mightn't that reduce profits?

Yes, particularly in the mining industry, where you're digging a hole the size of the harbour to yank some bauxite out or something. You can't do that without doing a bit of burning.

And you've got to keep mining going of course.

Of course I do. I'm the Minister for the Environment.

It'd cost jobs, wouldn't it, if we reduced greenhouse emissions?

It would. We can't afford to do it.

One adult in three is on a benefit in this country already.

Good God! One in three? When did this happen?

Now. That's the position now.

One in three?

Yes.

We'd better burn some more fossil fuels.

Will that help?

Yes, that's what I was arguing for in New York. If we reduce greenhouse gas emissions we'll lose jobs.

So if we can increase them, we'll get more jobs.

It's worth a try.

Have you talked about this with John Howard?

He's very, very concerned about all this, of course.

Have you discussed it with him?

No, he was at the cricket.

Who's behind all this reduction nonsense?

Well, the European countries are very keen on it for some reason.

On saving the world?

Yes, they're obsessed. You should have heard Tony Blair and Helmut Kohl. You'd think saving the world was the most important thing on earth.

What about in our region?

Oh. We couldn't give a toss.

I meant in the Asia-Pacific.

Well, there are some islands in the Pacific that are disappearing, but nothing serious. We're all right.

Why are their islands disappearing?

I've got no idea. I'm the Minister for the Environment.

These are the people who say the sea is getting higher.

Yes, but I've heard of the high seas before. I used to read about the high seas when I was a kid.

Aren't they saying that the greenhouse emissions heat the atmosphere and the polar ice-caps melt?

I don't know. Not really my area. I'm the Minister for the Environment.

Don't you get information coming in about this all the time?

Oh I don't open my mail.

Why not?

John Howard was at the cricket.

Thank you for your time.

He normally wouldn't open it himself. But he wasn't there.

So *you* didn't open it?

I didn't even admit it had arrived.

Thank you.

I'm the Minister for the Environment.

THE HON. JOHN HOWARD
PRIME MINISTER OF AUSTRALIA

Mr Howard, thanks for coming in.

Pleasure.

I wonder if I could ask you: do you think Australians are racist?

No, I don't but (oh blast, I've got to stop doing that).

What's the problem?

I keep sticking a 'but' at the end of my sentences. I must try to stop
doing that.

Do you think you *can* stop doing it?

Well, I'd like to think so, but...

**What's the problem with saying 'but' at the end of everything you
say?**

Well, it undermines everything you've just said. You can say something
perfectly reasonable. You can say what you meant to say. You can say
what you think is appropriate...

You can say what you know very well you ought to say.

...yes, but (bugger it).

**As Prime Minister, I suppose sometimes you've also got to say what
you think the people of Australia would want you to say.**

Yes...

Careful.

...but (blast).

Have you tried just not saying anything?

Yes, but...

But you can't.

No, I can't. Some people are good at being brief, at saying just enough,
at judging exactly how much to say and stopping there but...

Some people are quite good at expressing themselves.

Yes they are, but...

But you're not one of them.

Yes I am, but...

Don't you have speech writers?

Yes, I do, but…

Was this the problem in Melbourne at the Reconciliation Convention?

No. There's another problem there. We've got to get the people who are going to Pauline Hanson concerts to come back to the Coalition.

Do you agree with what Pauline Hanson is saying?

No, but (blast).

Why don't you speak against her?

I do…

Watch out.

…but…

Mr Howard. What were you being asked to apologise for?

To the Aborigines.

Yes.

For a whole lot of things that have been happening to them for the last two hundred years.

Since *we* got here.

Yes, but we didn't do it.

Look, I might be able to help you out here. These things that have happened to the Aboriginal people. What were they?

Oh, it varies. It's not even the same in each case. In some areas they were wiped out. In some places they had their land taken away from them. In some cases we gave them diseases. In some cases they had their children taken off them.

Did all these things happen?

Yes, of course they did. But I didn't do them.

Hang on. Did they happen? Forget about who did it. Did it happen?

Yes, it did, but I repeat, I didn't do it and neither did Pauline Hanson.

Mr Howard, didn't you just have to express the view that you were sorry it had happened?

Yes, but…

It doesn't seem impossible, does it?

It's all right for you. You're not speaking from where I was speaking at the time.

Where were you talking from?

But.

You were talking out your butt?

Oh, God. Now *you've* got it.

THE HON. PHILIP RUDDOCK
MINISTER FOR IMMIGRATION

Mr Ruddock, thanks for joining us.

Pleasure.

I'd like to ask you about this decision to reduce immigration.

Only by immigrants.

Pardon?

We're only cutting down on the number of *immigrants* who can come
into the country.

From overseas.

We believe that's where they're coming from, in the main, yes.

So other than immigrants, anyone can come?

No, no one else can come. I haven't made myself clear. You can't
come into Australia if you're not an immigrant. You've got to be an
immigrant to get in. That's what an immigrant is.

So you can't come at all if you're not an immigrant.

That's right.

**And you're cutting down on the number who can come because they
are immigrants.**

Well, they won't be immigrants now because we're not going to let
them in.

No, but they'd be immigrants if you'd let them come here.

No, they'd be Australians if we let them come in, but we're not going to.

Mr Ruddock, you're not making sense.

How dare you. I'm the Minister for…

Letting people in.

Keeping people out.

Who are you letting in?

Well, we let you in.

I was born here.

We're not preventing people who were born here from coming in.
You've got nothing to worry about.

Why would you prevent people who were born here from coming in?

Yes. That was our feeling. *(He is suddenly distracted and speaks in an urgent whisper.)* Is that Pauline Hanson? In the other studio. Hello Pauline.

Mr Ruddock.

It is. It's Pauline Hanson. Stand up.

Pardon?

Have some respect. Get up.

Mr Ruddock. You say this decision has got nothing to do with Pauline Hanson.

Nothing whatever, no. Hello there.

What are you going to do next?

Don't know. I don't know what she's saying. See if we can find out what she's saying. You never know what she's going to say.

Why do you need to know what she's saying?

So we can make a decision that's got nothing to do with that either.

Do you agree with what Pauline Hanson is saying?

I don't know what she is saying. I can't hear her.

Do you agree with what she's saying generally?

No I don't. Certainly not. Hello Pauline. Philip Ruddock, Canberra.

Well, why don't you make a stand against her?

Because I don't wish to dignify her comments by entering into a discussion with her. I've met her you know. I've actually met Pauline Hanson.

If you don't want to help her, why are you waiting to see what she says before you make your next policy announcement?

So that we as a government can continue to be completely uninfluenced by her unrepresentative, poisonous, racist policies.

Oh, she's looking over here. Look at that. She recognises me. Philip Ruddock. Good morning.

She's writing something for you. She's going to hold it up.

No, I can't send Aborigines out dear. I'm only in charge of who's coming in. I'm sorry, I can't. Yes, I agree with you dear but…

You said you didn't.

Shut up, I'm talking to the Prime Minister.

THE HON. JOHN HOWARD
PRIME MINISTER OF AUSTRALIA

Mr Howard, thanks for your time.

Pleasure.

You've been meeting with Meg Lees almost every day since we last spoke.

I have, yes.

And how has it gone?

Very well. What a nice person.

She is a nice person, isn't she?

It was most enjoyable.

What actually happened?

We sat down. We spoke in a general manner.

What did you say to her?

I explained that I was in a spot of bother. Needed a bit of a hand.

A bit of advice?

Yes. I ran it past her in broad outline.

How did you describe the problem?

I said I was running a democracy.

What did she say?

I tell you what, she's got a very good sense of humour.

Likes a laugh?

Oh, she's wicked.

Did you actually say you were running a democracy?

Yes.

Don't the people run a democracy?

And you reckon she didn't pick *that* up?

She's quick.

Doesn't miss a trick.

Did you explain what you'd done?

Yes. She asked me for a bit more information.

What did you tell her?

I said I'd brought in a policy people didn't want, without consulting them on the detail. And without having the numbers in the Parliament.

Is this conversation recorded?

Yes. It's all official. There are minutes and so on.

Are there?

Yes. It's like Hansard. Here are the minutes from yesterday, I was just checking through them.

Can I have a look?

I don't see why not. I'm planning to be out of the country when the tax comes in.

(He reads.) **'The meeting began at 10:22.'**

It's good, isn't it? What does it say next?

'Mr Howard asked Meg Lees whether she had considered his offer.'

That's right.

'Ms Lees asked whether this was the same offer he had made a week previously and which had been rejected on approximately three hundred and twelve separate occasions.'

'Mr Howard sought some guidance as to the precise number of times it was necessary to repeat a statement in fairly simple English in order for its delivery to be effective.'

'Ms Lees requested clarification as to whether or not perhaps there was some flannel or heavy towelling material impeding the passage of sound through Mr Howard's aural passages.'

'There was some speculation from Mr Howard as to Ms Lees' apparent incapacity to distinguish between the lower reaches of her torso and her elbow.'

'Ms Lees suggested a brief adjournment at this point which would provide Mr Howard with an opportunity to see an ophthalmologist.'

'In an attempt to break the deadlock Mr Howard ventured the opinion that it might be an excellent idea if Ms Lees were to avail herself of the education system and in particular the aspects of it whose job it is to accentuate the knowledge of the broader public in the area of economics.'

'Ms Lees asserted that this was a privilege already vouchsafed to her and she expressed some surprise that a detailed knowledge of

macroeconomic reform in its many aspects was a part of the training normally available to small-minded suburban solicitors.'

'Mr Howard asked whether or not there was any point in continuing with this conversation, richly textured and enlightening though it undoubtedly was.'

'Ms Lees concurred and suggested that should Mr Howard have a brief period over the next couple of hours when he wasn't being instructed what to do by big business or Treasury, he might like to go out into the street and see how much photochemical smog was being produced by diesel engines.'

'Mr Howard attempted to disavow Ms Lees of the view that he had arrived in conjunction with the previous shower.'

'Ms Lees named a prominent religious figure and offered a detailed suggestion about the exact placement of the GST as outlined.'

'It was agreed that the meeting would reconvene after lunch.'

What's this here about food?

That's just a note to myself, for our next meeting, to make sure we've got something to eat.

Why?

All through the meeting she wanted to get takeaway food.

Really?

Yes. Takeout food. She kept saying it over and over.

THE HON. TIM FISCHER
LEADER OF THE NATIONAL PARTY

Tim Fischer, thanks for your time.

Good to talk to you, Bryan.

You must have been pleased with the response to your decision to get out of politics.

Yes. I have been affected by the warmth of the response, yes, both from colleagues...

And from who else?

No. They were both from colleagues from memory.

You're being given a fair old send-off in the media, aren't you?

There are some very fine journalists in Australia. I think it's one of the things we do best.

Let's go back over some of the events of your time in politics, because it's been an interesting time, hasn't it?

It has. I wouldn't have missed it for quids.

You were elected in...what?

I was elected in New South Wales.

Yes. What year?

1999.

So how long were you in there?

I've got no idea. My watch is in the glovebox.

No, I'm asking about the period since you were first elected into Parliament.

Oh yes, you're not allowed in if you're not elected, that's the way it works.

When was that?

Yes, no doubt about that at all.

Just reading from tomorrow's paper here...

I'm in tomorrow's paper?

There's very little else in it. It's mostly you, tomorrow's paper.

Did they use the photos?

Yes, here you are in the army...

Yes, that's me.

What's this here? This is you being a statesman, is it?

No, I'm just wearing a hat.

It says here 'Tim Fischer: The Statesman'.

That must be the car. I'm just standing there in a hat.

Here you are splitting the atom.

No, I'm just wearing a hat again. Here I am going for a swim, look. That's up the bush.

Yes 'Tim Fischer: The Great Australian' it says here.

Great Australian?

Yes.

That can't be right. I voted for a GST.

Here's one of you with a store dummy.

Where?

Here. You're showing an R. M. Williams store dummy a sheep.

That's John Howard.

No. That's a sheep.

This other one here. That's John Howard.

What's he looking like that for?

He's trying to look like an Australian.

Why?

He's going to bring in a GST.

Will you miss the cut and thrust? Do you think?

Two questions there.

Let's take the first one. Will you miss the cut and thrust?

No. I'm getting out before they introduce a GST.

But you helped bring it in.

Exactly. I'm not a complete idiot.

Well what's this then?

That's me in the hat again.

Mr Fischer, thanks for your time.

Gidday. I'm Tim Fischer. How are you?

THE HON. ROBERT HILL
MINISTER FOR THE ENVIRONMENT

Senator Hill, thanks for your time.

Very good to be here.

You must be pleased.

Yes, indeed.

To have Kakadu listed as a uranium mine.

It's a great result. We're very proud.

Good for Australia.

Australia didn't do it. *We* did it.

I mean it's good for Australia that it happened.

You've lost me.

Is it tough to get a site listed as a uranium mine?

Yes, it's quite a detailed process.

How do you do it?

First of all you've got to get elected.

How do you do that?

You adopt a lot of policies you think people will like.

Like what?

Like envirotuninal policies.

Environmental policies?

That's them.

You're the Minister for the Environment.

Of course I am. I just turned part of it into a uranium mine.

So you get into power with your environmental policies. And then what do you do?

You do what you like once you're in.

This is why we're increasing greenhouse gases?

Yes.

And turning a national park into a uranium mine?

Not the whole park.

A park with a uranium mine in it?

Yes. Nice big park. Few trees. Shrubs. Herbaceous borders.

And a uranium mine.

Australian industry at work.

You won't be able to drink the water.

Why not?

It'll be poisoned. That's what happens with a uranium mine.

The miners will take the water with them.

Is it a beautiful place?

Not really. It's a big hole in the ground full of trucks and bulldozers.

I mean Kakadu.

Kakadu? It is now, yes.

You don't think it always will be?

We've given an international undertaking to turn it into a uranium mine.

You've promised?

Solemnly.

Mr Hill, thanks for your time.

This is a Howard Government promise.

THE HON. JEFF KENNETT
PREMIER OF VICTORIA

Mr Kennett, thanks for your time.
Good evening.
You've called an election.
For the eighteenth of September.
During the footy finals.
Yes, there'll be a show of hands at half-time in the preliminary final.
And you're confident?
I hope I'm not over-confident. There's always a chance something will go wrong in this type of thing.
In an election?
Anything where people are given a choice, yes.
There's always a chance they'll get it wrong?
There is, sadly, yes. Mistakes happen. They've happened before.
They have. You're spending twenty-four million dollars on education.
No, we're not.
If you get in.
If we get in we will, yes. We're certainly not doing it at the moment.
Have you got the money?
Are you kidding? The economic management of this state is probably the best in the country at the moment.
Things are going well?
We're rolling in it. Haven't you seen the accounts? We've been rolling in it for years.
Why aren't you spending twenty-four million dollars on education at the moment then?
We will if we get back in.
It's needed, is it?
Yes, the education system in Victoria is falling apart.
Why?
I forget why.
Bad teaching perhaps?

No. Can't be that.

Why not?

We fired the teachers.

How's the health system going?

You've lost me. The expression 'health system'?

Back to education then. Why haven't you done something about it?

We're going to.

If you get back in.

I can't do anything about it if we don't.

But if you've got the money, why don't you do it now?

Are you reading the questions properly?

No, I threw away the questions you gave me.

What are you reading now?

I wrote my own questions.

That's smart. Where were you educated?

I was educated before you got in.

THE HON. BRONWYN BISHOP
MINISTER FOR AGED CARE

Bronwyn Bishop, thanks for your time.

What a pleasure it is.

I wonder if I can talk to you about your performance over this nursing homes issue?

It's not just my performance, Kerry. I have a whole department of other people who don't know what's going on either.

I'm not Kerry, I'm Bryan.

If you'll let me finish, Kerry. The fact remains that I am simply the minister. I'm simply the minister responsible. None of this is my fault.

Minister, are you satisfied with the standard of care in Australian nursing homes at the moment?

I'm satisfied with it in some cases and not in others.

Can you be more specific?

Yes, I'm satisfied with it in the case of those nursing homes I've never heard of but I'm a great deal less satisfied with it in the case of the ones I've managed to find out anything about.

Are you happy with the performance of your department?

Look, it's a very hard job.

What is?

Whatever it is they're supposed to do. It's tough. I couldn't do it.

How do you know that?

I don't even *understand* it. These people have got to *do* it.

What do you take 'ministerial responsibility' to mean?

I'm not here to discuss theory, Kerry. There's not much point in that at this time. We've got a lot of older people in some of these places.

We have to do something about the standard of care, don't we?

This is a very practical problem. Let's work out a solution. What the minister has got to do is get in there and *fix* it.

You *are* the minister.

Exactly. Let's get on with it. As soon as those facts are presented to me I'll be on the case like a ton of bricks.

How will you do that?

We will look at any complaint as soon as we are made aware of it.

How would you be made aware of a complaint?

Someone would write to us.

They have.

Historically, yes, but just let me finish, Kerry. They would write to us, documenting the nature of the complaint and detailing the facts involved.

And then you would act?

Hang on, Kerry…

…Bryan.

Hang on, Kerry, you've asked me a question. No, we would not act yet.

I'm sorry. What would happen next?

The letter would be referred to the right people.

Who would it be referred to?

I don't know who is involved but that would take approximately three months.

And then the letter comes back?

Not always, no.

But sometimes.

On the odd occasion, yes, the letter might come back.

And then you would know about it?

Not necessarily.

Why not?

We mightn't be there when it came back.

Why wouldn't you be there?

I could be anywhere. I might be in the Parliament. I might be out looking at a nursing home. The standard of aged care in this country is a disgrace!

Can it be improved?

It has to be. These people can't look after themselves, some of them have worked all their lives, served their country overseas, raised families. It's very important that we let these people have their dignity.

How will you do that?

I'll round up some television cameras and visit a few of them.

Thank you, minister.

You may touch my raiment, Kerry, but only briefly.

THE HON. JOHN HOWARD
PRIME MINISTER OF AUSTRALIA

Mr Howard, thanks for your time.

Good evening, very good to be with you.

Mr Howard, how many policies do you have on Aboriginal affairs?

Do you mean in town or in the bush?

Let's look at the 'in town' ones first.

In the city, or in the regional centres?

In the cities.

In an election year or just normally?

All the time, ideally.

An all-the-time, work-for-all-cases Aboriginal policy?

Yes.

I'm afraid I don't understand your question.

Let me put it this way. Can you explain the business of mandatory sentencing?

Certainly. Do you know what mandatory sentencing is?

No, that's what I want to ask you.

OK. Do you know what 'mandatory' means?

It means obligatory.

What does obligatory mean?

Obligatory?

Is it Irish?

Not O'Bligatory. Obligatory.

Where is it? Is it up in the Territory?

It's a bit like 'unavoidable'.

Ah yes. Mighty pretty country round there. I was up there recently.

You were in the Northern Territory?

No, but I was up that way.

Where were you?

I had to go up to Pymble for a meeting.

Mr Howard, why is the United Nations being critical of Australia at the moment?

I don't know. I've been trying to work that out. This has got nothing to do with the United Nations.

What hasn't?

The treatment of Aboriginal people in Australia.

The UN has said they haven't got basic human rights.

The UN has got no business criticising us at all.

Why not?

Because we support them. We helped write their human rights charter.

They have a human rights charter?

Yes, the member countries of the United Nations formed a charter years ago.

Are we a member of the UN?

A very important member. Doc Evatt wrote a fair bit of the UN charter.

And what is the purpose of the UN human rights policy?

To prevent governments from acting in a way which would threaten the lives of their own citizens.

Would that happen?

It has. Look at East Timor.

That was tragic, wasn't it?

Sometimes a government is so bad, so bereft of what the broader world would accept as a basic standard of moral responsibility to its own citizens…

…That it will simply ignore the plight and condition of sections of its own people?

Yes.

And what might happen?

Many of them will die.

So the UN seeks to protect the fundamental human rights of those people?

That's the idea.

And if it doesn't, who will?

Exactly. If the UN doesn't say something about the condition of these people, their privations and their distress might continue.

These are genuinely appalling governments you're talking about, aren't they?

They are. I'm citing the extreme to highlight the UN policy and its importance.

So what is our objection to the UN's criticism of us on this issue?

It's none of their business when it happens here in Australia.

Do you mean 'What right do they have to speak about what's going on in an individual country?'

I do. We're running Australia. The United Nations isn't running a country.

Doesn't it represent all the countries?

Yes, but there's a difference between what you'd like to happen and what actually happens in the real world. It's like going to church. You go to church on a Sunday, you listen to a lot of stuff about what you ought to do, how you ought to live your life…

You agree.

Yes, you agree. That's why you've gone to church.

But you don't act on the principles you've expressed your support for.

No, you wouldn't need to go to church if you lived like that anyway. You'd be out there doing it.

So what is Australia's position on human rights? We support the UN charter on human rights?

We support the UN charter on human rights, but we are opposed to the UN charter on human rights.

Hang on, Mr Howard. You can't say that. It doesn't make sense.

Doesn't it? Are you sure?

You just said, 'We support the UN charter on human rights, but we're opposed to the UN charter on human rights.'

I see. I can't be on both sides.

That's right. It doesn't make sense. Do you want to answer the question again?

Yes. Ask me again.

Mr Howard, do we support the UN charter on human rights?

In theory, yes.

But not in practice.

We support it in practice in Timor.

But not south of Timor.

No.

We support it in the Gulf.

But not in the Gulf of Carpentaria.

Do we support it in the Falklands?

Yes, but not in the other rural electorates.

THE HON. MICHAEL WOOLDRIDGE
MINISTER FOR HEALTH

Dr Wooldridge, thanks for your time.

Nice to see you. Sit down. What seems to be the trouble?

You've created a bit of a furore with your remarks about tampons, which attract the GST because they are, of course, a luxury item.

Yes, well, I've apologised for my remarks.

Why did you apologise?

I got told to. John Howard rang and told me to apologise.

Why did he say you had to apologise?

Apparently I'd upset a whole lot of people.

Who were they?

I don't know. Some minority interest group somewhere.

Women?

That's it. That was them, yes. I don't know who's organising them.

You don't know who women are?

Yes. I know who women are. I'm a doctor.

You're trained to tell the difference.

Oh yes, it's one of the first things you learn.

But you didn't recognise them as a political grouping?

I didn't realise they were working together, no.

I don't think they were, were they? Until you united them.

I've provided them with a point on which they all agree?

Yes.

That's certainly the thrust of a lot of the emails we've been getting.

That you're a little p…?

Yes. That I'm just a little patronising.

Have you done it before?

The tampon routine, 'I beg your pardon, I didn't know menstruation was a disease.'

Yes. The comparison with shaving cream.

Oh, I've done it plenty of times. I'm a doctor. It normally works pretty well.

It's pretty funny, isn't it?

I think it's funny, yes, and as I say it normally goes gang busters.

Who is your normal audience?

I'm a doctor.

So mostly blokes.

Yes. And a lot of women who want to marry doctors.

They'd find it funny.

Oh, they are the greatest audience.

They'd pick up everything I suppose would they, the women?

Not if they look after themselves they won't.

How are they going to look after themselves?

Yes, we're getting a lot of emails about that.

THE HON. JOHN HOWARD
PRIME MINISTER OF AUSTRALIA

Mr Howard, thanks for your time.
Well, very nice to be with you, thank you.

I wonder if I could ask you about the huge turnout for Corroboree 2000?
Yes, certainly. What was the name of the team again?

Corroboree 2000. You know, the reconciliation movement, the walk across the bridge?
Ah, yes, I recall something of the type.

Did the enormous response surprise you?
No, not really. I'm speaking from memory…I think I spoke at it, didn't I?

Yes, you did. You had the opportunity to apologise too, didn't you?
This was the thing where a whole lot of people were given the wrong map.

A faulty map?
Yes, they were obviously under the impression I was going to be giving a speech from the rear of the hall. They were all facing the wrong way. Every time I looked up…

They had their backs to you?
All I could see were the backs of people's heads and lots of hats.

Maybe the acoustics were bad?
Frankly, I didn't like the look of any of them.

Mr Howard, did you see the speech as an opportunity to offer an apology?
I saw the speech as an opportunity to express some concerns I think a lot of people have about apologising for something that they didn't do.

But the apology that's required isn't about your personal responsibility for what happened.
That's good, because I haven't done anything wrong.

Isn't what's required, Mr Howard, an acknowledgment that what happened did happen?

Well, look, if something happened, obviously somebody did it. And it wasn't me!

You don't have to be the one who did something to feel sorrow for the people it happened to.

Good, OK, can we talk about something else now? Much though I have enjoyed the thrust of your early questions.

Mr Howard, you recently went to the battlefields of France?

I did, yes. I visited a number of Australian graves and…

You said you were sorry that they'd lost their lives.

It was a tragic loss of life, absolutely tragic.

Did you kill them?

I beg your pardon?

Did you kill them?

No, of course I didn't kill them. What do you mean, 'Did I kill them?'

How can you be sorry for something you didn't do?

Oh, this is completely different.

Why is it different, Mr Howard?

Well, you yourself said this was in France. It's not even in Australia. It's a completely different country. It's off the coast somewhere.

Do you think anyone actually agrees with you on this issue? There were a lot of people on the Sydney Harbour Bridge.

Plenty of people agree with me.

Who?

Well, look, my wife's brother works with a woman whose husband is a mechanic at a hospital. The person who runs the hospital, his sister knows a bloke who agrees with every aspect of what I say about this really rather complex question.

Can we ring him?

Certainly, we can ring him. I was talking to him earlier.

And he agrees…

He agrees absolutely with everything I say.

OK, it's ringing.

(Howard's phone rings.) Excuse me for a moment. Hello?

Hello. Mr Howard.

Yes, can I ring you back, mate? I'm just doing an interview. *(He hangs up.)*

Who was that?

I don't know, but don't worry about him.

Why not?

The GST'll get him.

THE HON. JOHN HOWARD
PRIME MINISTER OF AUSTRALIA

Mr Howard, thank you for your time again.

Good evening.

Mr Howard, are you going to amend the legislation on sexual discrimination?

Yes, we are.

Isn't that an area where the states have legislative control?

It is.

I thought you were opposed, as a federal government, to overriding the states?

We *are* in the instance of mandatory sentencing, of course, but not on this issue.

The issue of IVF treatment?

That's right. In-vitro fertilisation. 'In vitro' simply means 'in glass'.

Oh, so they do it in a test tube?

No, you can't do it in a test tube. A test tube's rather a small thing. As a general rule you need room to take your hat off.

I meant the fertilisation takes place in the test tube.

Oh, I beg your pardon, yes. That's all done by people in white coats.

So what is the issue here, Mr Howard?

The issue is quite simply this: who has access to IVF treatment?

And who has the right to stop them?

That's right. Somebody's got to stop them.

Aren't there already decision-making criteria in place to cover these questions?

There are, but I don't agree with them and I'm going to change them.

Mr Howard, didn't the court decide that your criteria were sexually discriminatory?

They did. That's right. That's why I'm going to change the rules.

Who's going to have access to IVF treatment under your legislation?

Women who are married.

Or are pretending to be married?

Yes, that'd do.

Or behaving as if they're married?

Yes, with any luck.

Women who'd like to be married?

Yes, girls with a few brains.

Not single women and gay people?

No, that's what I'm not having! I'm not having that. *I'm not having that!*

OK, Mr Howard, settle down. Can I just throw a couple of other groups at you?

If you must.

Married child molesters?

No. Child molesters will not have access to IVF treatment.

What if you don't know they're child molesters?

In that case, how can you prevent them?

What about people who are living together when they get the IVF but not afterwards?

That would be unfortunate, but it'd probably be all right.

How would they get the IVF back if you didn't approve?

Exactly. You can't.

What would you do to them?

Oh, I don't know. Jail the mother?

What about people who don't like their children?

Are they married?

Yes.

No problem there.

You said a child within our society had a right to the care and affection of both mother and father.

I did, yes. That is my belief.

How are you going to make that happen?

In the case where there's only one parent you can't, obviously.

What about the case of two parents?

Well, you can't, again, obviously. Those are the only two areas, though, where that argument has any weakness at all.

What about a tree?

A married tree, this is?

Yes, a married tree.

Yes, no problem there. That should be OK.

Sheep?

Married sheep, these are?

Yes.

That can be very successful. This proposal went pretty well in Cabinet, for example.

What happened?

I told them it wasn't a matter for their conscience and they were to get through the gate quick-smart.

Mr Howard, thank you.

(Scribbles.) Thank you. Here you go. Any chemist will make that up.

article   discussion   **edit this page**   history

Abbott and Costello

Tony (Ears) Abbott and Peter (The Smirk) Costello performed together as **Abbott and Costello** and were an important part of the act known as The Howard Government (also known as The Follies). Ears played the talkative dumb one who made a fool of himself in revolving doors and The Smirk played the other talkative dumb one who pretended to be 'a contender'. Would he take control? Would he leave the stage? Would he sing? Would he dance? If anyone gave a toss, would the toss attract a tax?

Their most popular routine was 'Who's on First?'—full of rapid-fire word play, confusion and frustration and ultimately not about anything. Hilarious.

THE HON. PETER COSTELLO
TREASURER OF AUSTRALIA

Mr Costello, thanks for your time.

Good evening, it's very nice of you to invite me on the program.

Mr Costello, are you happy with the new Cabinet?

Absolutely. A very good Cabinet, some very good people in there.

Some exciting, fresh new ideas?

Are you still talking about the Cabinet?

Yes. Are you pleased with the economic position?

Australia's economic outlook is very strong. Very strong indeed.

That's good.

It is good. It means we can get on and rebuild the surplus.

I was going to ask you about that. What happened to the surplus?

Didn't we have a huge surplus at one time?

We did, Australia's economic management in recent years has really been…

Pretty spectacular.

…something of a triumph, yes.

So where's the surplus?

Well, we had one or two expenses. I mean, we've had a refugee crisis to…

Generate.

…deal with. And that was a very, very…

Cheap trick.

…expensive exercise and, of course, we've also undertaken a lot of new programs in the light of…

The need to get re-elected.

…the need of the broader community.

Mr Costello, why aren't we still under threat from the asylum seekers?

I'm sorry. Are we not?

We don't seem to be. It's not in the paper these days.

Oh really? I must get out more.

I thought they were coming down here in their thousands.

That was certainly my impression.

So where are they now?

Well, I gather from what you seem to be saying that since the federal election the asylum seekers have found us a lot less attractive as a destination.

Or maybe it's not in the papers as often?

Yes, although why that would be, I don't know, do you?

Maybe they've stopped throwing their children overboard.

Hang on. I don't know if we actually knew they were throwing their children overboard exactly.

No, but we were told that they were.

We were told that it had been reported, that there was a possibility that in certain instances it may have been a possible construction, that elements of overboard-throwing had occurred in some specified nautical areas at that time.

We were told that by the Minister of Defence, weren't we?

He didn't say it had happened. He said it had been reported that it had happened.

Yes, but in what capacity did he say it had been reported that it had happened?

In his capacity as the defence minister.

A most reliable authority.

It was Peter Reith.

Yes, but even so.

We're getting out of my area slightly. Can I just say that I can't answer questions about directly what happened up there. I wasn't there. I was actually very, very busy here.

Doing what?

Trying to work out how to pay for it, young man.

Mr Costello, thank you for your time.

Don't thank me, son. Wait until you see what it cost.

THE HON. DARYL WILLIAMS
ATTORNEY-GENERAL OF AUSTRALIA

Daryl Williams, thanks for your time.

It's very good to be here, thank you.

Attorney-General, we're having a lot of problems up in Woomera at the moment, aren't we?

We have been experiencing one or two problems in the Woomera area recently, yes. The people being held in detention there are engaging in what I would describe as acts of destruction.

Wanton destruction.

'Acts of wanton destruction', yes.

Why are the people being held there?

These are people who are waiting for their applications for refugee status to be processed.

And why don't they like being in a jail in Woomera?

I've got no idea.

Is it a nice place?

It's a beautiful place, an absolutely beautiful place. It's got walls.

A roof?

Roof, yes.

Fence?

A beautiful fence. It's got one of the best fences I think I've ever seen in my life.

Really? Any trees?

No trees. But a fantastic fence.

Flowers?

Flowers, no. The fence is a ripper, but there aren't any flowers.

Just walls and roof and the fence?

Yes, an absolutely beautiful fence.

Is it near anything?

The building?

Yes.

Yes. It's very near the fence.

I mean, are there towns nearby?

No, this is a detention centre. It's not a hotel we're talking about.

Is there a visiting area?

What's a visiting area?

You know, a place for people to visit people.

No, nobody's going to be visiting these people. It's in Woomera.

And what do these people want?

They want to have their applications processed and get out.

And become part of the community?

That's right. But they're not going to do that so long as they behave in the way in which they have been. They set fire to the place. We're not going to be intimida—

What would happen if they stop causing problems at the detention centre?

What they've got to understand is that they must stop these acts of wanton destruction. They've got to cease being vandals and settle down.

And what will happen if they do?

If they do, we can then look at the possibility of perhaps engaging in some discussion that might ultimately move towards an application review of some kind, at some stage, in respect of some of these people. And actual processing may result in some instances.

But minister, isn't that the problem? Isn't that the reason for their actions? That we're not processing their applications?

We're not going to process anything at all under any circumstances, if they keep behaving in the way in which they have been.

Aren't they behaving like that purely because you're not doing these applications for them?

We will refuse to process anything so long as people are acting like this. That's what they've got to understand and that's what I'm indicating to you.

OK. And what happens if they do stop?

If they don't stop, we're not going to process anything. That's the position.

And if they *do* stop?

Unless they stop, nothing will happen.

So we'll hear their applications if they *do* stop?

We won't be hearing anything unless they stop. That's what I'm saying to you.

Yes, but if they stop, will we process their applications for them?

Let me put this another way. The way to get us to hear their applications is to stop doing what they've been doing. They've got to stop behaving like vandals.

They've got to stop engaging in acts of wanton destruction?

Wanton destruction, yes. Your term. They've got to stop doing that.

But if they stop the acts of wanton destruction, will we process their applications?

Not if they keep behaving the way they have been.

Daryl Williams, thank you very much.

Thank you. I just wanted to clarify the government's position.

THE HON. JOHN HOWARD
PRIME MINISTER OF AUSTRALIA

Mr Howard, thanks for your time.

It's very good to be with you. Thank you for inviting me in.

I wonder if I could ask you about the babies overboard business?

Yes. Certainly. The story that's coming out now or the story we told at the time?

The story that we're getting now.

This week's story?

Yes.

The Monday story? The Tuesday story? Or the one that's broken subsequently?

Well, perhaps today's story.

Today's story?

Yes.

This morning's story or the one we're using now?

What's the difference?

The point I'm making is I have no intention of discussing the period when Peter Reith was saying one thing and I was saying another.

Neither do I. That's fine.

Look, please don't interrupt. I'm trying to answer your question with honesty and integrity…

Both of them?

Simultaneously, yes. And you're interrupting. That's not very helpful.

OK, I'm sorry.

Neither have I any intention of discussing the period when Peter remembered that he was told it wasn't true but he'd forgotten to tell me.

Why would he have neglected to do that?

Don't interrupt, please. It's not helpful at all.

OK, I'm sorry. Go ahead.

Then of course we had the period when Peter thought he may have told me that the thing was completely untrue but he didn't tell me in English.

Oh, that's right. I remember that. Yes, yes, yes. How long did that version last?

It didn't last very long.

It was almost subliminal, wasn't it?

I don't think that was one of our better ones. Then we stumbled on what I believe is an absolute cracker, which was that we were all grossly misinformed by an incompetent public servant.

Public servant. That's the current version, isn't it?

What's the time?

7:55.

Yes, that's still current, I don't think we've found any involvement that Peter Hollingworth may have with this issue as yet.

So what does he do now, Peter Reith?

Since he retired from Parliament? Peter was lucky enough to secure employment negotiating government defence contracts. *(Laughs.)*

(Laughs.) **Really?**

Yes. *(Laughs.)* I'm sorry. I'll try that again, sorry. Just ask me that again.

So what does he do now, Peter Reith?

Since he retired from Parliament, Peter has been lucky enough to get a job negotiating government defence contracts. *(Both parties doubled-over laughing, desperately trying to compose themselves.)*

Sorry, that is very funny.

I'm sorry. I apologise.

Can I do it again? So what does Peter Reith do now?

Since he retired from politics, Peter… *(fighting back laughter)*…I'm sorry. It took us four hours to get this right in the Cabinet room before we could even…

OK. You look that way and I'll look this way. *(They face different directions.)*

Yes. Now ask me again.

So what does Peter Reith do now?

Peter Reith, at the moment, is…*(Explodes with laughter.)*

Maybe we'll move on. Let me ask you another question. Why do you

think people would throw their own children into the sea?

Why would anyone believe that parents would throw their children in the sea? That's too hard. Ask me the Peter Reith one again.

OK, all right. So, Prime Minister, what does Peter Reith do now?

Peter Reith has got a job selling government defence contracts.

(Both parties erupt into laughter.)

SENIOR BANKING EXECUTIVE

Thanks for your time.

Take a number, will you? I'll be with you in a minute.

You're one of Australia's leading bankers.

Yes. Just take a number, son. I'll be with you as soon as I possibly can.

How many banks do we have in Australia?

There are three or four of us operating in what is technically described as the banking sector. We're all in—what's that thing called?

Sydney.

No, no. It's in the paper all the time.

Russell Crowe?

No. It's where there are only a few of you and you're pretending there are quite a lot of you and you actually control everything.

Competition?

Competition! We're all in competition with one another.

So why have you closed my branch?

Is this an inquiry?

Yes.

Inquiries down the end there, son.

Well, is there anyone else I can speak to?

Someone else in the bank?

Yes.

No.

Why not?

He's at lunch. Do take a number. I'll get to you as soon as I finish doing this.

But hang on, who am I supposed to talk to?

Is this an inquiry?

Yes.

Inquiries down the end there, son.

It would be a lot easier, actually, if you could just answer my question.

Are you on the internet?

No, I'm not.

What you do is you go on the internet and you go to our website…

But I'm not on the internet.

You've got to be on the internet to go to our website.

But I don't want to go to your website.

You can't do your internet banking without going on the internet. You need to go to our website.

Look, excuse me, I don't want to do my banking on the internet. I want to go and do my banking at a branch.

Yes, well just take a number, son and go down there. I'll be with you as soon as I possibly can.

There's no one down there.

No one down at inquiries?

No.

But there will be when you go down there.

No, I mean there's no one working down there.

That's right. We're a bank, son. We're not here to provide light entertainment. How are we going to make a quid out of answering a lot of silly questions?

Listen, I can't do my banking because you shut my branch and I want to know why.

You want to know why we shut your branch?

Yes.

That's an inquiry. Take it down to inquiries.

Where am I supposed to do my banking?

Are you on the internet?

Is this an inquiry?

Of course it's an inquiry. I'm trying to find out if…

Inquiries down the end there.

There's no one there. I'm trying to help you, son. You want to know how to do your banking?

Is this an inquiry?

Of course it's a bloody inquiry.

Inquiries down the end there.

I give up.

Yes, I worked that out. My question is where do I do my banking?

I'm sorry, I'm afraid all our usual methods of avoiding the issue are currently engaged. Your call has been placed in the toilet.

THE HON. JOHN HOWARD, PETER COSTELLO AND SIMON CREAN

Right. Buzzers working. John Howard?

Buzz.

Peter Costello?

Buzz.

Simon Crean?

Buzz.

Right. OK. If you were letting the market run the economy and the market fell over, what would you do?

(No one answers.)

Are those buzzers working? John Howard?

Buzz.

Peter Costello?

Buzz.

Simon Crean?

Buzz.

We'll go on to the next one. If you deregulated the financial markets and took away all the rules, what rules would then govern the behaviour of the financial markets? *(No one answers. Bryan talks to the director.)* **Shane we've got a problem here. Are these buzzers working?**

Yes.

Are those buzzers working? John Howard?

Buzz.

Peter Costello?

Buzz.

Simon Crean?

Buzz.

We'll try another one. If you went into business to make a huge amount of money, and you had to give your shareholders anything that was left over, why would there be anything left over? John Howard, you must know the answer to this.

Can I phone a friend?

Yes, let's phone a friend. We're dialling the number now. Hello?
(Peter Costello answers.) Hello?
No, John, you can't call Peter. *(Turns to next question.)* Here's one you'll all get. What is superannuation?
Buzz.
John Howard?
Smaller?
Buzz.
Peter Costello?
It used to be an amount of money you put aside for when you retired.
Good, but I want to know what it is *now*.
Buzz.
Simon Crean?
Is it something to do with the 60/40 Rule?
No, Simon. Final question. General question. What is humanity?
Buzz.
John Howard?
The guy who runs Western Mining?
No, that's Hugh Morgan.
Buzz.
Peter Costello?
Is it something to do with Philip Ruddock?
No, I'm afraid it's not.
Buzz.
Simon Crean?
Is it when there's no opposition?
No, that's Australia. *(A new person enters.)* Hello? Who are you?
I'm Ray Williams.
And what's your problem Ray?
Buzzzzzzzzzzz.
(All buzzers buzz forever.)

THE HON. JOHN HOWARD
PRIME MINISTER OF AUSTRALIA

Mr Howard, thanks for your time.

Pleasure.

This last year has brought about a huge change in the way Australians regard regional security, hasn't it?

It has. There's been a loss of innocence.

Yes, when did this happen? Could you date this for us?

I think it began just before the last election.

Going back, take us over what you've said.

I've tried to best represent the interests and concerns of the Australian public.

But take us back to when all this started. Australians were all living happily here...

Yes.

Minding their own business...

Yes.

And so what did you do?

I yelled out that there was a wolf coming.

Was there a wolf there at that time?

No, but Peter Reith informed me there was a wolf.

Where was he saying the wolf was?

He said the wolf was in the water.

A wolf in the water? What would a wolf be doing in the water? Wolves aren't found in the water are they?

These wolves were.

According to Peter Reith.

That's right.

And then it turned out they weren't there at all?

As it turned out, yes.

What happened next?

George Bush announced he was going to conduct a war on Iraq.

What did you do when that happened?

I did what I was told.

Yes, but what did you actually say?

I said I'd seen a wolf.

Did you yell this out?

Well, I went on television and said that I'd seen a wolf.

Another wolf?

Yes.

This time in Iraq?

Yes.

You'd seen a wolf in Iraq. And how would you have seen a wolf in Iraq?

I didn't actually see it. George saw it.

And how did you know George had seen a wolf?

He rang me up and shouted 'wolf' down the phone.

'Wolf in Iraq'?

Yes.

So now you'd said you'd seen two wolves.

The one in the water and the one in Iraq, yes.

And how many had you actually seen?

Strictly speaking?

Yes.

I hadn't seen any.

And then what happened?

Then we got attacked by a wolf.

This was in Bali?

Yes, that's right.

And did you see that coming?

No. We had no warning of any kind.

And what were you doing at the time?

I was very busy at the time.

Doing what?

I was on television trying to describe the wolf I'd seen in Iraq.

The wolf you *hadn't* seen in Iraq.

Yes, well, both of them really.

Which both of them?

The wolf I hadn't seen in Iraq and the wolf I hadn't seen in the water.

So whose fault is all this, do you think?

The wolf's. Let's be quite clear about that.

Of course, Mr Howard.

It was all the wolf's fault. *Look out!*

THE HON. PETER COSTELLO
TREASURER OF AUSTRALIA

Mr Costello, thanks for your time.

Very good to be with you, Bryan, very good indeed.

Well, you're out selling the Budget. What's the reaction from the flock?

It's going very well. The flock are pleased and I think it's broadly seen as a very sensible and responsible Budget.

And they'd have to be happy with a tax cut?

Yes, you put $513 per week in their kick and they won't complain too much, will they?

Who is getting that again?

If you're a forty-five-year-old male politician from Kooyong with a wife and family, you're getting $513 in your pocket per week extra—more than under the twelve Labor Budgets put together.

The Iraqi war cost Australia a lot, didn't it?

Well, I think you've got to face facts, Bryan. If you're going to invade another country, it's going to belt your projections around a bit.

Now, the higher education package, can you explain that to me?

Certainly. At the moment, the way the system is, and we're just adding just a mere thirty per cent to this, if you go to a university there are two ways you can pay. You can pay full fees, Bryan—

Up front?

Yes, full fees, that is.

And how much does that cost?

Well, it depends on what course you do.

Say a three-year course?

Yes, a nice little bottom of the range product. About forty gorillas.

Gordon Bennett!

Or else—What's his name?

Gordon Bennett.

Gordon could perhaps pay using the old H.E.C.S. method, which we're replacing with another one—

Lay-by?

Yes, lay-by, yes. Nice easy terms, see one of our friendly staff, Bryan.

And how does Gordon pay it back?

He pays it back later when he's earning a quid and kicking on rather well.

And you charge interest?

Only a bit.

So what would he owe on that?

Well, if Gordon paid this back over perhaps five years, we might be into him for about 45K.

Gordon Bennett! What if he did law or medicine?

Yes, by all means. Are his parents doctors or lawyers?

I don't know.

He won't be doing law or medicine if his parents aren't doctors or lawyers.

So the only people who can do law or medicine are people who have parents who are doctors and lawyers?

Well, if we've got the projections right, Bryan, on those figures, that's where the landing lights are, yes—

So why make them do the course in the first place?

I see. If they're the only people who can do the course, why bother running the course!

They'd pick it up at home, wouldn't they?

Good point, Bryan. Of course we'd have to subsidise that, but we'd be able to do that with the money we're yanking out of the education budget—Good point.

What about the people whose parents aren't doctors and lawyers? There must be a few of those?

People who go to university and have not got a parent who is either a doctor or a lawyer?

Yes.

Yes. Well, have you read the Budget documents?

Yes.

Well, they're going to be nurses and teachers, aren't they?

Gordon Bennett.

Let me be clear, Bryan. We're not opposed to the mongrel class going to university, they're just not getting into the professions.

And what's it called again, this scheme?

H.E.L.P.

THE HON. PETER COSTELLO
TREASURER OF AUSTRALIA

Sit down, Peter. *(Peter sits down.)* **What's the matter?**

Nothing.

Can I ask you a few questions?

All right.

You don't seem very happy.

I'm all right.

What happened?

Nothing.

Come on, I heard all about it. What happened?

Johnny wouldn't give me a go on the bike. He'll never give me a go on the bike now.

Did he say he would give you a go?

Yes, but he won't. He'll be on it forever. He'll never get off it now.

Hang on. What did he actually say?

He said he'd give me a go.

Didn't he say he'd *think about* giving you a go?

Yes, but he won't. I'll never get a go on the bike now.

Look, I'm sure he'll give you a go.

When?

When he's ready.

I want a go now. He said I could have a go now.

Johnny's having a go now, and he's pretty good at it. I've seen him going past my office a few times.

You should see him when he's not going past your office. He doesn't even tell the truth. He tells big whoppers about what's going on.

Johnny doesn't tell the truth? What are these big whoppers he's been telling?

If I tell you what the big whoppers are, he'll *never* let me have a go on the bike.

But if you don't tell us what the big whoppers are, you'll be helping him tell the big whoppers.

Yes I know. Bloody Johnny.

He's snookered you a bit here, hasn't he?

I hate Johnny.

Come on, you don't hate him. You're just a bit angry.

I'm bloody furious.

We all get angry from time to time. Look on the plus side. Johnny lets you play with the accounts, and there are people who say you're really not very good at that.

I only got one thing wrong.

Yes, but it was rather a big thing, wasn't it?

No, I only put the wrong price in for Telstra.

But you could have got the right price, couldn't you?

How?

It was in the paper, wasn't it, Peter?

I didn't have a paper.

So what did you do?

I made a price up.

So it looked as if there was a surplus?

Johnny told me to do that. That was Johnny's idea to have a surplus. Bloody Johnny, I hate Johnny.

Look, let John have his turn and then when he's finished, you'll get to have a go. And I'm sure you'll be very good at it too.

I should have had a go a long time ago.

You'll have a go.

Thanks for coming to see me.

That's all right. Feel a bit better now?

Not really.

Mark William Latham

Mark William Latham (born 28 February 1961) was the sole British entrant in the 1988 Winter Olympics ski-jumping competition. He had previously competed at the 1987 World Championships, and was ranked fifty-fifth in the world. Mark turned up with borrowed equipment and had to wear six layers of socks to make the boots fit. He was handicapped by his weight—he was heavier than any other competitor—and by his lack of financial support. He was also very short-sighted, requiring him to wear his glasses at all times, even though when skiing they fogged to such an extent that he could not see. He was also afraid of jumping. 'Of course I was. There was always a chance that my next jump would be my last.' He finished last in both the seventy metre and ninety metre events.

However, his lack of success endeared him to people all across the world. The worse he did, the more popular he became. He was leader of the opposition between December 2003 and January 2005.

MARK LATHAM
PREVIOUS OPPOSITION LEADER

Mr Latham, thanks for your time.
Nice to be with you, Bryan. How are you?

I'm good, thank you.
Good on you, Bryan.

Gee, you've cut quite a swathe this week.
I don't know about a swathe, Bryan, but I've certainly cut a bit of a swathe during the week.

It's a tough business, isn't it, politics?
I don't know about tough, Bryan, but I'll tell you something about this business, it's pretty tough. Pretty tough.

Didn't you know it was going to be tough when you went into it, though?
Yes, yes. You don't go into a business like this, Bryan, without knowing it's going to be tough. I knew it would be tough. I knew it would be tough. I knew it would be tough.

Did anything surprise you about it, though?
Only the toughness, Bryan. Only the toughness.

But you would have expected that, wouldn't you?
I did. You don't go into a business like this, Bryan, without knowing what to expect.

But were you surprised when it turned out to be so tough?
I wasn't surprised in the sense that it surprised me.

It's just that you didn't expect it?
Exactly. Exactly. Exactly, Bryan. Exactly.

Mr Latham, when did you first realise they were all against you?
When they made me leader of the Labor Party.

And who did that?
They all did. The whole bloody lot of them. They all got together, all of them, literally all of them. And they ganged up on me. They made me the bloody leader of the Labor Party.

And did you expect that?

Well, not to the extent that it happened, Bryan, no.

Did you want to be leader of the Labor Party?

Well, I was in the party forever, Bryan. I've been in the party for years and years and years and years and years and years and years and years.

A long time?

So in a way it was kind of an honour to lead these scum.

So you were proud?

I don't know about proud, Bryan, but I tell you something, it makes you proud when it happens. It makes you proud when it happens.

And who was there when they chose you?

Well, there was a bunch of us there. There was me, Dinsdale Piranha and a bloke called Kierkegaard who just sat there biting the heads off whippets.

Kim Beazley?

Beazer was there. Wayne Swan was there. Good to see Barry Hall in the team, isn't it? Good to see Barry got off. Isn't that good news?

Yes. Different sort of Swan, though.

Yes, but it's good to see a bloke getting off a charge of clouting people. I reckon that's quite good.

Oh, you like that?

That's the Australian way for my money, Bryan. That's the Australian way, isn't it?

Mark Latham, thank you very much for your time. Good luck with the book and thanks for coming in.

Yes, well, you can start any time you like now, Bryan.

Pardon?

Ready to roll when you are, Bryan.

We just finished.

Yes, but you don't know what you want to say until it's all over, do you? It doesn't matter until it stops mattering. You don't know what you're going to say until you finish doing the stuff. *(Looking away.)* You see that bloke over there?

Yes.

That's me.

(Concerned for Mr Latham's health, Bryan wraps it up.) **Right. Thanks for your time.**

THE HON. JOHN HOWARD
PRIME MINISTER OF AUSTRALIA

Mr Howard, thanks for your time.

Pleasure.

You've announced a three hundred and sixty-five million dollars early childhood package.

Yes I have, Bryan. A very important initiative of great benefit to Australian families.

Yes. What is it?

Works out at a million dollars a day. Three hundred and sixty-five days, three hundred and sixty-five million.

Yes. How does it work?

Yes, hang on. I've got this written down somewhere.

The opposition has dismissed this as a pre-election bribe.

They would, wouldn't they.

Why?

Because we announced it in response to their pre-election bribe they announced the other day.

So theirs is a pre-election bribe but yours isn't?

Here you go. 'This is based on the twin concepts of social cohesion and early intervention.'

What does that mean?

That means those are the two central elements in the plan.

Social cohesion and early intervention?

That's right. Cohesion. 'Co' meaning 'with'; co-venture, co-operate, co-mbine.

Combine?

Yes. To join something with something else.

Cohesion?

With hesion.

With hesion?

Yes.

There hasn't been enough hesion?

There has been insufficient hesion, Bryan, in early childhood for some time.

And early intervention. What does that mean?

That means not intervening too late. There's no point in intervening too late. If you're going to intervene too late you might ask yourself whether it's worth intervening at all.

In what?

In anything. This is the thing about intervention.

If you're going to do it, do it early.

That's the key point.

Yes, but why intervene at all?

In early childhood?

Yes.

We believe it's the best way to get in there and make sure there's enough hesion.

What exactly *is* hesion?

I don't know. This would all be done by experts.

Hesion experts?

Hesionologists will be airlifted in, Bryan, into those areas of early childhood.

Where the hesion has been lacking?

Where there has hitherto been a paucity, yes, of hesion.

Mr Howard, can free trade be explained like this?

There are some problems with logic and free trade.

Why?

Because it's not free and there are certain respects in which it's not trade and we're not entirely sure it's going to happen at all.

What about aged care?

Look, I'll be right. I've got parliamentary super.

Thanks for your time.

Precisely.

THE HON. ALEXANDER DOWNER
MINISTER FOR FOREIGN AFFAIRS

Alexander Downer, thanks for your time.

It's a great pleasure, Bryan, and good evening.

Can you explain the position of David Hicks to us, please?

Yes, indeed. The David Hicks case is one I'm very familiar with.

He's an Australian citizen arrested by the Americans in Afghanistan.

He is, yes.

And what has he been charged with?

He hasn't been charged with anything yet, Bryan. But I'd say he's obviously guilty.

Guilty of what, Mr Downer?

Yes, good point. He hasn't been charged so he can't be guilty of…

How long has he been in jail, Mr Downer?

He's been incarcerated for, I think, about nineteen months.

In Cuba?

In the Caribbean, Bryan, yes. Have you ever been up there?

No, I haven't.

It's a lovely spot, the Caribbean. It's an absolute cracker. If you're ever given the opportunity, I'd whistle up there quick-smart.

I'll make a note of that. Mr Downer, has David Hicks seen a lawyer?

I doubt that he would have seen a defence lawyer.

But he would have seen a prosecuting lawyer?

He may have seen one or two prosecution lawyers, yes.

A Cuban?

I would think an American in his case.

Mr Downer, is that fair?

From what I understand, Bryan, he's lucky to see any bloody lawyer at all. He was training with al-Qa'ida. He was training in the use of weapons with al-Qa'ida.

Mr Downer, who told you that?

The Americans, Bryan. I'm not a fool. I've spoken to the prosecutors.

But he hasn't been tried yet, has he? How long is he going to be

there? That is my point.

He's obviously guilty, Bryan.

You keep saying this, but guilty of what?

I don't know what he's being charged with, Bryan, but what I'm indicating to you is he probably bloody did it.

(Sighs.) **Mr Downer, are you familiar with the trial of Roger Casement?**

Roger Casement?

No? Doesn't ring a bell?

It's not an Adelaide name, Bryan, no.

Roger Casement was a citizen of one country, he was kidnapped in that country, taken to another country and then tried for treason in that second country.

He was taken from one country, removed to another country and tried for treason in respect of that second country, which wasn't the country he came from?

Correct. And then executed.

Executed! Good Lord.

Do you see any similarities?

Yes, I do.

Like what?

Guilty as buggery, the pair of them, Bryan.

A 'MASTERMIND' CONTEST

Your special subject is John Howard. Your time starts now. What will John Howard never bring in? Ever.

A GST.

Correct. When did John Howard bring in a GST?

The first of July, 2000.

Correct. What are weapons of mass destruction?

Sorry. Is that George on the phone?

Correct. If you know people want a republic, how do you get them to vote against it?

You ask them to vote for a republic where they don't get to vote for the President.

Correct. What is the Kyoto Agreement?

Something to do with coal prices?

Correct. What is the environment?

Pass.

Correct. What were being thrown overboard into the sea just before the last election?

Nothing.

I beg your pardon. I misread the question. What did John Howard *say* **were being thrown overboard into the sea just before the last election?**

The children of asylum seekers.

Correct. What did he do to prove it?

He released a film of it not happening.

Correct. Who told him the children *were* **being thrown in the sea?**

The Minister for Defence said he'd been told by the navy.

Correct. And what did the Minister for Defence do when the navy denied that?

He resigned and got a job selling defence contracts to the Australian Government.

And was there a conflict there?

No. It was Peter Reith.

Correct. What about some of the other people in the Howard ministry. When they've retired, where have they retired to?

To jobs with companies who operate in the fields where they used to be the minister.

Correct. And would this have been worked out beforehand?

Shut your face.

Correct. What does the word 'integrity' mean?

Can you repeat the question?

Correct. If you make a promise and don't keep it, what was it?

A non-core promise.

Correct. Who can get married in Australia?

Marriage is between a man and a woman.

What if they don't like each other?

It doesn't matter if they hate each other's guts as long as one of them is a man and one of them is a woman.

Correct. Why don't we have to listen to senior members of the defence community criticise the government on defence?

They're too old.

Correct. Why don't we have to listen to ex-public servants criticising the government's use of research information?

They're the scum of the earth, public servants.

Can you be more specific?

Get stuffed.

Correct. And at the end of that round your house is worth three times what you paid for it.

Great.

Congratulations.

Thanks. Three times what I paid for it!

Yes. Low interest rates. You're worth a fortune.

He's great, John Howard, isn't he?

Correct.

THE HON. BRENDAN NELSON
MINISTER FOR EDUCATION

Brendan Nelson, thanks for your time.

Just relax, Bryan. Pace yourself.

You've announced plans to get stuck into the universities.

We've announced plans to reform certain aspects of the tertiary education sector. You see this is where the ABC gets itself into trouble. There's no need to ask that question in that form. I don't know why you do it. It gives you away. You've got an ideological position. You're pretending to be objective. You're working for the national broadcaster.

Who do you work for?

I'm in a different position. I work for the government.

Mr Nelson, I…

No, let me finish, Bryan. You're a public servant. The ABC is owned by the government, by the taxpayers. Ordinary people paying their tax, that's where your bread and butter comes from. Your job, if I might say so, is not to express your own particular poisonous prejudice. It is to make the program in the best interests of the whole of Australia, this is the Australian Broadcasting Corporation.

I understand that.

Well that's good.

May I continue?

You may, but bear in mind the guidelines I've given you.

Certainly. And I thank you for the tips.

Pleasure.

Dr Nelson, you've announced plans to reform certain aspects of the tertiary education sector.

That's right, Bryan, I have.

How are you going to achieve this?

What does it mean in practical terms?

Yes.

We're going to get stuck into the universities, Bryan.

Yes. Why is that, Dr Nelson?

It's ideological. There are ideas being expressed in the universities at the moment that are not the government's.

Hasn't that always been the case?

It has, Bryan. It's taken us a while to wake up to it but we're on to it now.

Are there other places where there are ideas being expressed which aren't the government's?

Outside the universities is the other main venue for dissent.

You believe that the universities should be controlled by the federal government?

I do. *(He looks to the back of the room.)* Who is that giggling? Come on. Share the joke.

Dr Nelson. You've said you don't think university students should have to join a student union.

That's right. I don't think the Australian public wants its money spent on a lot of radicals running about the country doing as they please. *(He looks to the back of the room.)* Who said that's what taxpayers are doing? Who said this government is a bunch of radicals who aren't acting in the best interests of the country? I can wait. I've got all day. This has happened before, hasn't it?

Not since you were here last.

We'll wait, Bryan.

Are we staying in?

Yes. You can bang the dusters together. Come on. Bang bang.

THE HON. ROBERT HILL
MINISTER FOR DEFENCE

Senator Hill, thanks for your time.

Pleasure, Bryan.

You've had a bit of a problem with the accounts in the defence department.

Let's be clear about this. The accounts are quite good. A model of their kind.

What kind are they?

Accounts with eight billion dollars worth of assets missing.

There are no rural grants in these accounts are there?

No, not at all. These are just the accounts of the Australian defence establishment.

So what's the problem with the accounts?

The problem isn't with the accounts.

So where would an accounting problem be if it weren't in the accounts?

I'm only the minister responsible but it would be in knowing where the things in the accounts actually were.

The assets.

The alleged assets.

Like what?

Defence equipment. Have you seen the Budget?

Yes, I've got a copy of it.

If you go to the capital expenditure, you'll find the ordnance is all listed there.

This is the equipment.

Yes. It's all listed under specific headings.

'Things that go "whoosh"'?

Yes. Good example.

'Things that go "kerblam"'?

Yes, different class of weaponry.

'Things that go AWOL'?

They're in a separate schedule.

Where is it? Is it here?

No. We don't know where that is but it'll turn up, it'll be somewhere.

'Helicopters we ordered four years ago'?

Yes.

Six hundred million dollars.

Yes.

Each.

That's right.

Why does it say 'No photo available'?

Because we haven't got the helicopters yet.

We've just paid for them.

That's right. That's the key point. As soon as we get them we'll be out there with the camera.

So these items listed as being 'probably somewhere'?

It's more specific than that, isn't it?

Yes. Sorry. 'Probably somewhere in Australia or Asia or the Middle East.'

Yes.

These are actual weapons are they?

Correct. Top drawer stuff too.

But we don't know where they are.

Yes. They'll be somewhere. We just have to find them.

How are you going to do that?

I've been given the name of some people who might be able to help.

Who are they?

There's a guy called Hans Blix.

The weapons inspector?

Yes. Apparently he can go into your country and find weapons.

And you're going to get him to come to Australia and find ours?

Well, we can't find them. We must be practical.

What are they?

The missing items?

Yes. Eight billion dollars worth of what, exactly?

Items defence personnel have mislaid.

What sort of thing?

Some submarines.

Someone's mislaid a submarine?

Yes. Just put one down somewhere.

And forgotten it?

Yes, the phone rang or something.

How do you think the taxpayer feels about all this?

The taxpayer should be very happy.

Why?

The quality of the stuff we can't find is second to none.

Senator Hill, thanks for your time.

You haven't got some amphibious tanks have you?

No. Why?

(*Looking around.*) Anyone? Amphibious tanks? Rockets?

THE HON. KIM BEAZLEY
LEADER OF THE OPPOSITION

Thanks very much for your time.

Very good to be here. Good evening.

You are…Mr?

Kim Beazley.

Kim Beazley. That's right. How are you? I haven't seen you for a bit.

No. I'm very well thanks. How are you?

I'm good thanks. Now you're doing the job of…

I'm the leader of the opposition.

Yes. Mark Latham's old job.

Yes. Mark's no longer with the firm.

Where is Mark now?

Mark's working from home.

Who was in Mark Latham's old job before Mark Latham?

The way we look at it, it's not Mark Latham's old job. It's my job.

Yes, but who was in the job before Mark Latham?

Simon Crean was.

And before that?

I was, before that.

And before that?

Before me?

Yes.

Me again. But look, you seem to be concentrating on the past. We're
a party of the future. We have a forward-looking view…aren't you
going to interrupt me?

No, I was going to see what you had to say.

I haven't got anything to say. I was just making the point that we're the
party of the first part…

(Helping.) **Of the future.**

Of the future.

**My point is that you go back a fair way. You were the last leader but
two and the last but three.**

That's right.

When were the Crusades?

The Crusades were before that. My position is similar to that of John Howard. He had about six goes at being leader before he won an election.

And why was that?

The Liberal Party was shell-shocked. They'd been humiliated in a few elections on the trot. They didn't know what they were…Didn't know how best to get the man obviously best suited to manage the country, into the driver's seat.

You nearly won the federal election in 1998, didn't you?

I did. I came within a…

A win.

I came within a win of winning that one.

And you came within a win of winning again in 2001.

I did. The only thing that prevented us from winning that one was the…

The fact that you had the same policies as the government?

Not so much that but that they had them first.

So you had some bad ideas?

We had plenty of bad ideas.

But you didn't have them first.

That's right, and that told against us.

Did you toy with the prospect of having any good ideas, at any stage?

Yes, I'm pretty sure we looked at that.

Wouldn't work?

I think someone suggested that. Perhaps some of the women.

You don't think it would work?

It wasn't up to me. I was only the leader of the party.

So who runs the party if not the leader?

I've got that here. (*He takes a card from his pocket and reads.*) A bloke called… Who's this? I didn't know there *was* a Rupert Packer.

That's two cards.

I see. *(Off.)* Harry, what's the name of the bloke who ultimately sets ALP policy at the moment. That's it. John Howard.

Thanks for coming in.

THE HON. PHILIP RUDDOCK
ATTORNEY-GENERAL

Mr Ruddock, thanks for your time.
A very good evening to you, Bryan.

I wonder if I could ask you about this new legislation that's coming in.
Yes, this is the anti-terrorist legislation?

Yes.
Yes, that legislation has been on the books for some time.

These are amendments, aren't they?
We are bringing in some amendments, yes.

And what is the purpose of them?
Well, we will be giving the authorities certain powers, Bryan, the better to defend Australia from terrorism.

What sort of powers, exactly?
They'll be able to enter premises, for example, where they think there might be terrorist activity.

And arrest people?
And arrest people, by all means. We hope they will, yes.

And what will they arrest them for?
Well, they might, for example, think they know something.

They might know what?
Something maybe they shouldn't know, Bryan.

What sort of thing?
That's not specified in the legislation. This would be a matter for them.

So, they could arrest me?
Theoretically, Bryan, yes, if they thought you perhaps knew something.

What sort of thing would I know?
As I say, Bryan, this is not specified in the legislation. This would be a matter for the arresting officer.

But, Mr Ruddock, how would I establish my innocence here?
Well, you wouldn't be innocent, Bryan, if you were being arrested, would you? They are not going to arrest you if you are innocent. They're not fools, these people.

How do I get out of this?

You'd have to establish, in some persuasive way, that perhaps the thing that they thought you knew, you don't know.

How do I do that?

I have no idea, Bryan. That's not my problem.

But I would have to prove that I didn't know it.

That's it. It's fairly simple.

But isn't that the opposite of the presumption of innocence?

Bryan, this is not a normal situation.

In what way isn't it a normal situation, Mr Ruddock?

Someone has come into your house, Bryan, and arrested you because they think you might know something.

Yes, and it's up to me and I have to prove that I don't know it.

That's correct. It's not a normal situation.

Do they tell me what it is that I don't know?

No, they're not going to tell you what it is.

Why not?

Bryan, if I came into your house and arrested you because I thought you might know something, I wouldn't be able to tell you what it is without impeding your capacity to argue that you didn't know what it was.

In that case perhaps no arrest should be made until the alleged offence can be established, Mr Ruddock.

We don't want them to know. We're not going to tell them, Bryan.

But if you don't tell them what it is, how can they possibly argue that they didn't know it? They don't know what it is, Mr Ruddock.

That's right. I think you'll find we've got them there, Bryan. I don't think they've got a leg to stand on, myself, and they deserve everything they've got coming.

When is this legislation coming in?

After 1 July, when we don't have to trouble the scorer much. We'll run both houses.

And you wrote this?

I'm not alone, Bryan. There were several of us there.

Who?

Oh, there was me, Lewis Carroll, a bloke called Escher from South Australia; a few of us.

Do you know what I think of this legislation, Mr Ruddock?

Be a bit careful here, Bryan.

Do you know what I think of this legislation?

Be a bit careful what you say.

(Public announcement.) Bryan Dawe, to the front desk, please. There are some gentlemen here to see you.

Don't look at me, Bryan. You got yourself into this.

A NEWSPAPER EDITOR

Thanks for your time.
No trouble at all.
You run what I suppose we can call a major daily newspaper.
Certainly. One of the big four.
Which are the big four?
Ourselves and the three other big ones.
And how are things going in the media at the moment?
They're going pretty well. Advertising revenues are up. We're
certainly going well.
And what are the big stories at the moment?
The big news stories?
Yes.
You've got your Danish Prince and Princess…
This is Mary, the girl from Tasmania?
Yes, our Mary. A fabulous story.
It is a great story, isn't it?
It's a dream story. It's got elements of reality and fantasy.
He seems so nice too, doesn't he?
He does. Everyone likes him. A marvellous story.
And they've been in Sydney of course.
They have charmed Sydney.
Yes. What else?
Well yes, there are other stories of course. You've got your Danish
royals. They're in Melbourne now.
**Yes, I mean apart from the Danish royals, what other stories are big in
Australia at the moment?**
Plenty of other stuff; Prince Charles, Delta, someone hacked into Paris
Hilton's phone, we're doing a thing on where to get the best coffee,
shoes…
What's happening in the Middle East?
House prices, yes, they certainly seem to have stabilised.
No I mean in Iraq.

Iraq?

Yes.

Something about Syria.

Yes, what about Syria?

I think George Bush has warned Syria.

What about?

Warned them to stop doing that thing they were doing.

What will he do if they don't stop?

I imagine he'll go in there and bring freedom and democracy to the Syranians.

How do you think the Australian economy is going?

It's going well. As I say, advertising revenues are up. We're making a poultice…

I mean the broader economy.

Advertising revenue is up across the board. I don't know anyone who's not making a quid out of advertising revenue.

Do you think there'll be another interest rate hike?

Not before Gallipoli. We've pretty much got the Gallipoli coverage organised. They'd be mad to get in the road of that.

How do you think the poor are travelling in this country at the moment?

The poor? Look, I'll be honest, we don't cover a lot of stories about the poor.

Why not?

It's difficult to interest the advertisers in buying space in a story about the poor.

What about the sick? The health system doesn't work.

Yes, not news really if it's not working.

Or the aged?

No, you can hook them in on the old folks if there's a nice retirement development being released. 'Calming Vistas', 'Autumnal Heights' or something.

And what would you run there?

We wouldn't just be running the press handout, if that's what you're asking.

What would you be running?

We'll be running the press handout, but you can just cut at my last answer.

This is live.

We're going out live?

Yes.

(Off.) Get me a big picture of Prince Frederick and Our Mary, will you?

THE HON. JOHN HOWARD
PRIME MINISTER OF AUSTRALIA

Mr Howard, thanks for your time.

Nice to be talking to you.

Yes, there's been some discussion about Anzac Day this year, hasn't there?

Yes, there has, Bryan, and I've made my position as plain as I can get it. I support those Australians who were there at Gallipoli. I don't have a problem with their behaviour. I was proud to be their commanding officer.

Mr Howard, I was actually meaning the meaning of Anzac Day altogether.

I've seen it said that they perhaps got on the turps and left some crap lying about on the peninsula, but they are Australians. I mean, you get with your mates, you have a couple and lose track of what's going on and you make a bit of a bloody mess. We do that at home, Bryan. I don't see the difference.

Mr Howard, I wondered if the meaning of Anzac Day has somehow changed?

Anzac Day is a day of great importance in the Australian calendar, Bryan.

What do you think that importance is?

Well, I think the essential lessons and characters of Anzac Day are as they have always been, Bryan.

And what are they?

Well, it celebrates that very important time when the Australian Government made a very significant decision, Bryan, to…

To do as it was told by an imperial power.

…to assemble a very, very impressive body of young men, very talented, very resourceful young men and to send them away to…

Invade another country.

…to defend Britain.

By invading Turkey.

And the way they did it, Bryan, was of the utmost importance because for a start they were…

Landed in a wrong place.

…as I say, a very resourceful group of people. When you try to get into the AIF in the very first lot of volunteers, Bryan, you couldn't get in if you were under six foot one so, obviously our…

Graves were a little longer.

…army was a very impressive body of men and they were led by generals who were…

On a boat a couple of miles off the coast.

…dealing with a pretty significant problem. I mean they had a difficult task. That terrain—I've been over the land, Bryan, and it's very difficult land. I've done that, and a lot of the generals at the time…

Hadn't bothered to…

…they weren't given that opportunity because they were obviously…

Tucking into a bit of dinner.

…trying to deal with the bigger picture and there was a bigger picture because Anzac Day doesn't only celebrate Gallipoli. I mean, the First World War, Bryan, is full of other…

Cock-ups.

…very, very famous battles and this is where Australia comes of age. This is where we stand astride centre stage and become a nation. I mean, obviously the empire is not there any more. We're in charge of our own destiny now. Now when Australia wants to know what it's doing in the future it certainly doesn't look to Britain. What we do now is…

Ring George.

…hang on, I've got to ring George. I just got a message to ring George.

No, Prime Minister, that was me.

The important thing, Bryan, is that Anzac Day is very, very, very important to all…

Politicians.

Almost sacred, you might say, Bryan, to all…

Advertising sales.

…to all Australians.

Prime Minister, thanks for your time.

Yes, good on you. Now bugger off, I'm going to talk to George, Bryan, about Australia. We'll let you know. *(Into phone.)* George, John Howard. Howard.

A MINISTERIAL REPRESENTATIVE

Thanks for coming in.

It's very good to be here. Thank you.

You're not Amanda Vanstone, are you?

Am I Amanda Vanstone? No, I'm not really.

I thought we had arranged to speak to Amanda Vanstone.

Yes, well, the minister is very busy and I've been asked to pop in here and fill in for her.

I don't think we were told that.

I'm telling you now.

But we weren't told beforehand.

Well, I can't help that, sunshine. I'm telling you now, though. I didn't know about it a long time ago myself, to be honest.

What happened?

I was in the office. I got a call from the minister saying would I get down here and talk to—are you Barry O'Brien?

Bryan Dawe.

Whatever—about whatever particular bee you've got in your bonnet tonight.

We asked the minister, Amanda Vanstone, to come here specifically and talk about reconciliation and the response was that she was going to be here and that she was keen to discuss these issues.

Good response, too, but something's cropped up. The minister is very busy.

Well, where is she?

Aside from anything else, she is the Minister for Popping Small Children in the Jail.

She said she would be here at ten to eight.

Yes but something has cropped up and I am here to deputise for her.

Well, where has she gone?

She is at a 'Bring and Buy' in Braidwood, a very important party function. She is yanking a number out of a hat at quarter to nine. She cannot be here!

So this is more important than Aboriginal reconciliation?

Barry, what I'm saying to you…

Bryan.

Mmm?

Bryan.

Whatever. What I'm saying to you is I'm here to help. Ask me any questions. That's what I'm here to deal with.

How high a priority for the government is Aboriginal reconciliation?

Is what?

Aboriginal reconciliation—how high a priority is it?

Oh, you know, pretty high.

Pretty high?

Yes, fairly high. I've heard it mentioned. I've heard the adults talking about it in the other room.

This is ridiculous. You are saying that you've heard reconciliation discussed in an office somewhere?

Yes.

You're not serious about this at all. You've got no interest in it.

Don't patronise me, Barry.

Bryan.

Don't patronise me…Sonny, because I am down here. I should be at a life drawing class. Do you think I like coming down here? There are plenty of people the minister could have sent along here who are much more junior to me in the department. Don't you tell me the minister is not serious about…

Aboriginal reconciliation.

Whatever.

Can you tell me what the minister thought of the remarks of the Governor-General this week and the remarks of the Governor of Western Australia?

She would probably have been in broad agreement with them, yes.

With whom?

Well, what's the difference?

(Off.) Shane, this is pointless. Well, how are you on immigration?

Well, give us a run. I can give you a personal opinion on immigration.

Why not? You're missing out on life drawing.

Exactly. I support the Irish guy, Peter O'George.

Petro Georgiou.

Him as well. With them both. I hope that they get a very good hearing in this community.

Really? Why is that?

Because they're going to get rolled in the Parliament. I reckon give them an airing now and we'll put the idea to sleep when it gets to the Senate.

Sorry about the life drawing class.

Well, bugger you, too.

THE HON. PHILIP RUDDOCK
ATTORNEY-GENERAL

Mr Ruddock, thanks for your time.
Words, Bryan, cannot express the joy I experience whenever I move among you.

You've taken some flack over this decision to bring in the terrorism legislation on Melbourne Cup Day?
Bryan, the Parliament is sitting on Melbourne Cup Day. It cannot be a surprise that it will be engaging in governmental business while it is sitting.

Yes. I think the criticism is that the government appears to be trying to hurry through contentious legislation while the media and the Australian public's attention is elsewhere.
I understand the nature of that criticism.

What is your reaction to that criticism, Mr Ruddock?
I don't agree with that criticism. I simply make the point, Bryan, that the Parliament is sitting on Tuesday.

And then the next day the IR legislation's coming in?
You bet it is, Bryan.

You don't think there's anything wrong with this?
There is nothing the matter with this whatever, no. These laws, which are new, are not a secret.

Well, no. What went wrong there?
The bastard who is the Chief Minister in the ACT put the bloody thing up on his website.

And you weren't very pleased with that?
I cannot tell you, Bryan, how pissed off I was that a person elected to public office in this country would willingly divulge what we were going to do to the public.

Is that not the democratic way, though?
It is a constitutional crisis of exactly the kind you describe, yes.

Well, Mr Ruddock, what can you do about it?
We will be taking advice on this issue, as we do on many issues, Bryan.

What advice will you be taking?

We will be taking advice of the kind we took when we put all those asylum seekers in prison.

Why did you take legal advice in that instance?

Because the Constitution, Bryan, provides that only judges may imprison people.

What did that advice say, Mr Ruddock?

I cannot reveal to you the precise nature of the advice.

What did you do as a result of that advice?

I got myself another portfolio.

No, I meant what did the government do?

The government argued that it was not putting people in prison.

What was the government doing?

The government argued—successfully I might say—that it was putting people in *administrative detention*.

What's the difference?

Administrative detention, Bryan, is two words.

Those problems are now over, aren't they?

They are not over, no. The immigration minister spends an enormous amount of time and many millions of dollars dealing with problems devolving from those issues.

What are those problems?

Problems relating to the appalling treatment of those people.

Which people?

The persons who were seeking asylum in this country.

When?

During the time they were in prison.

Mr Ruddock, thanks for your time. Have a great Cup Day.

My Cup Day, Bryan, will be significantly better than yours or my name's not Rumpelstiltskin.

A 'MASTERMIND' CONTESTANT

OK. Our next contestant. Your name is Peter?

Yes, that's right, yes.

What do you do, Peter?

I'm a treasurer.

A treasurer. My, that must be an interesting job, is it?

Yes, it can be a bit repetitive sometimes. I actually wouldn't mind becoming a prime minister at some point.

Well good luck, Peter. Your special subject tonight is right-wing incidents in the life of Christ.

That's correct.

Your time starts now. Name one right-wing incident in the life of Christ.

He threw the money lenders out of the temple.

Can you be more specific?

Yes. He went into the temple and there were money lenders there and he became very angry and tipped their tables over and told them they were usurers and threw them out; biffed them out of the place altogether; threw them out of the temple.

What I meant was, how was that a right-wing thing to do?

Yes, I see. It probably isn't, is it?

Can you think of anything else, Peter?

Yes. He fed four thousand people at one time by sharing food.

How much did he charge for that food?

No, he didn't charge for the food, Bryan. He shared *his* food. They were hungry and he broke up food. It was loaves and fishes. You've probably heard the story.

I know the story. I'm trying to find the right-wing element in feeding people who need food.

Yes, I see. There probably isn't one, is there? He healed the sick.

Yes.

But actually I think he probably did that for nothing. In fact, I think he probably did that because he loved mankind.

It's not really a right-wing mantra, is it?

It's not a *central* tenet of capitalism, the laying on of hands, no.

He made the lame walk, too, didn't he?

He did, and he forgave the people who killed him.

Did he stick any people in detention centres?

Oh, no, I don't think he would have approved of that at all. He got one bloke up from the dead. A bloke was dead and he made him walk.

This is Lazarus?

Lazarus. Yes. He healed him completely. I don't think he would have approved of putting people in a detention centre, no.

Peter, would you like to reconsider your special subject tonight; right-wing incidents in the life of Christ…

No thanks. I'll think of something, Bryan. I'll have to come up with something sooner or later.

Why is that?

Oh, for this other project I'm working on.

You've snookered yourself a bit here, Peter, haven't you?

No, Bryan. I know! He said at one stage it would be as difficult for a rich man to enter the kingdom of heaven as it would be for a camel to pass through the eye of a needle.

Oh, I'll have to check that with the adjudicator, Peter. Hang on. Can we accept that? Yes, sure. Hang on, I'll ask. Peter, what is your net worth?

(Peter is appalled and realises he cannot win.)

A 'MASTERMIND' WINNER

Your special subject is Australian Government policy. Your time starts now. Official government policy is to sell Telstra?

Correct.

Or to retain ownership of the half they still own?

Correct.

For two different prices.

Correct.

To the people who already own it.

Correct.

Against the wishes of the Australian public.

Do you mean all of the Australian public?

I mean the great majority. Australia is a democracy.

(Guessing.) Correct.

Did the government put any condition on the sale?

Yes, but they did it anyway.

Correct. What was the condition?

That telephone services be improved in the bush.

Correct. And did they improve the services in the bush?

Sorry, can you repeat the question?

Can you be more specific?

I can hardly hear you.

Correct. What did Telstra used to spend its money on?

On research and development in telephony.

What did it spend its money on in recent years?

On returning a dividend to shareholders.

Correct. Why is Telstra not worth as much money as the government thought it was?

Because it has missed the boat on the new developments in technology and telephony.

Correct. Why?

Because it didn't spend enough money on research and development.

Correct. Why not?

Because it's been spending its money on returning a dividend to shareholders.

Correct. Why can't the government force Telstra to provide a proper service to the Australian public?

Telstra's a public company.

Correct. Why can't Telstra concentrate on the services where the money really is?

Because it's run by the government.

Correct. Who is Telstra's biggest shareholder?

The government.

Correct. Why?

Because they can't afford to sell it.

Correct. Why did they want to sell it in the first place?

Pass.

'**To give Australians an opportunity to purchase a stake in this great national institution.**'

(Snorts.) That can't be right—it's completely stuffed!

Hang on a sec. *(Seeks an adjudication.)* **Tony, can we accept 'stuffed'?**

T: Bloody oath we can; we were opposed to it in the first place and now it doesn't work as a service and it's missed the boat as a company.

(Both.) **Correct!**

KEVIN ANDREWS
MINISTER FOR WORKPLACE RELATIONS

Mr Andrews, thanks for your time.

Good to be with you, Bryan. Good evening.

You've dismissed huge demonstrations this week against your IR legislation.

Yes, they were fairly predictable. We thought that'd probably happen.

Will they have any effect?

No, of course they won't. Ninety-five per cent of people went to work.

So we won't be doing any AIDS research in this country?

No AIDS research? Why not? I don't see…

Well ninety-five per cent of Australians don't have AIDS.

Bryan, my point is that the unions are an archaic, smokestack organisation. It's not surprising to me that their mode of expression is basically irrelevant.

What should they have done?

A touch of the forelock wouldn't have hurt, I'd have thought.

Mr Andrews, there's a fair old alliance against you in this. It's not just the trade unions, is it?

Bryan, can I have a private word with you? You've got a bit of a problem here. I saw you involved in these protests. You marched in the street the other day…

Like a lot of Australians who have concerns about what you're trying to do here.

Well, you're biased aren't you, Bryan? I'd rather talk to someone who's not biased on this issue.

So would I.

I am not biased. You think I'm biased?

Of course you're biased.

We're not biased. We're the government. We're the government of the country.

Of course you're biased. You're bringing in this legislation.

I wasn't running about in the bloody street the other day, protesting against what's going on in this country.

Yes, which also concerns me. You think this is all right.

Bryan, I know it's all right. We've shown it to the Business Council. They reckon it's an absolute cracker.

Why don't the churches think it's a good idea?

Because they're biased.

Why don't the social welfare bodies think it's a great idea?

Because they're biased. Why do you think employer organisations and the Business Council reckon it's such a pearler?

They're biased.

Oh don't be ridiculous, Bryan, they're the people who understand the economy best.

Mr Andrews, would you agree that the government's IR reforms take power away from the employees and give it to management?

That's a very broad generalisation.

It may well be, but is it true?

As it happens it is true but it's a very broad generalisation and I want you to understand its broadness.

Will there be a Fair Pay Commission for executives?

No, that's not what the Fair Pay Commission is, Bryan, it's not for executives. Why do you ask?

Because if people see executives paying themselves these obscene amounts of money and workers are having their conditions taken away from them...

...They might get biased, yes.

They might get very biased indeed, Mr Andrews.

It's a fair point, Bryan.

Will you do something about that?

We might have to do something about that.

What will you do?

Keep executive packages out of the paper for a fortnight until we've got away with it.

It's a pity Telstra announced they were firing twelve thousand people this week, wasn't it?

Yes, the timing wasn't terribly good, Bryan. Of course there's nothing the government can do. The government doesn't own Telstra.

And whose decision was that?

Bryan, I'm happy to talk about IR reform, but I'd rather talk to someone who isn't biased, do you understand that?

Exactly my position. Couldn't agree more. Thanks for joining us.

You're fired.

THE HON. JOHN HOWARD
PRIME MINISTER OF AUSTRALIA

Mr Howard, thanks for your time.
Pleasure, Bryan. Good to see you and thanks for inviting me on the program. *(The Australian National Anthem begins. Mr Howard stands.)*
What's that?
The national anthem, Bryan. I think we should stand.
Why is the national anthem playing?
Because Australia is doing so well. It's a terrifically successful country.
Mr Howard, it's hard to have a serious conversation while all this is going on.
You'll get used to it, Bryan. It's not everyone's cup of tea but it's the way we do things at the moment and it seems to work well.
It's a bit distracting this, isn't it? How do you concentrate?
I am concentrating.
Don't you find it a distraction?
I find it rather relaxing. People love it.
How are we supposed to have a sensible discussion about anything?
Normal business goes on all the time. I make announcements about government policy all the time.
That's what concerns me. They used to interrupt a Cabinet meeting if Australia won the Ashes. Now you don't interrupt sport to have a discussion about government policy.
Yes we do, Bryan.
No you don't, you announced your new IR legislation during the Melbourne Cup.
Yes, but we didn't bring it in until the Commonwealth Games.
Were you at the closing ceremony?
Yes, it was magnificent.
What did you especially like about it?
It kept the uranium deal we've done with the Chinese out of the papers.
And you've decided to restructure the board of the ABC?
Yes, we did that during the swimming.

Can I ask you about this cyclone that went through Queensland?

Larry.

Yes, why did it happen?

I don't know. It's weather isn't it, cyclones?

Have we signed the Kyoto Protocol yet?

I don't know. I'd have to check.

Who would you check with? You're the Prime Minister.

I'd need to check with the Minister for Selling Coal.

Can you just sign this, please?

What is it?

It's an acknowledgment that we had this conversation, that I asked you about environmental damage and cyclones.

Why do you want a signed document?

We don't want the government to say it wasn't told about the connection between global warming and weather change.

Why would the government deny it had been told something?

Do you know anything about how the international wheat trade works?

No, but I could ask Alexander Downer.

Why ask Alexander Downer?

He won't know either. He's very reliable.

What are you going to do when this music finishes?

They'll start the Anzac Day music any minute.

THE HON. KIM BEAZLEY
LEADER OF THE OPPOSITION

Mr Beazley, thanks for your time.

Pleasure. Good to be here.

Yes. *(Bryan relaxes. He smiles at his guest.)*

Would you like to ask me some questions?

No thanks. Just happy to have you here.

Why am I here if you don't want to ask me anything?

We need balance.

Balance?

Yes, balance in the program.

Balance.

The ABC is very concerned with balance.

What is balance?

I've got no idea. It's not a decision I make. It's upstairs.

Balance with what?

We've had the Prime Minister in a couple of times. We need to balance that out.

With me.

Yes.

How do I balance the Prime Minister?

You're still with the Labor Party?

Yes, I'm the leader of the Labor Party.

Yes. Even better.

So what do we do?

Doesn't much matter. How's the economy?

Hard to say.

The war in Iraq?

Very difficult to say. Not really our war.

Health? Education? IR? The environment? What are you doing?

I thought I might try to finish the crossword.

That's 'apathy'.

What is?

That one ending with a y.

Which one?

Six-letter word meaning 'laziness or want of energy'.

No, I've got that one.

What is it?

'Policy'.

Policy?

Apathy? Could be. So what's this one down here?

What is it?

He was *blank* to be elected into high office for a decade.

How many letters?

Ten.

Triumphant.

Oh.

What did you have?

Wilderness.

No, it ends in a t.

Why?

Because that one across is Green voters.

'A generation of disaffected young people'?

Yes. What have you got?

Bugger them.

That doesn't fit.

It does if you colour a couple of these other squares in black.

What's that big one running down the side?

'Reason given for the war in Iraq'.

Thanks for coming in.

Doesn't fit.

No, I'm thanking you.

Oh. Have you got a rubber?

A VOTER

Thanks for your time.

Thanks for inviting me in.

I wonder if I can just go through some of your responses to these questions.

Yes, which ones?

You're a voter?

Yes.

Where are you?

We're in Mortgage Vistas.

OK.

Up the Gearing Highway.

Whereabouts?

It's about an hour and a bit up there. You know where the Kiddies are?

Yes.

Through there and it's about another 2.5 per cent.

Near Dreamy Peaks.

Yes, you've gone a bit far there. It's between Dreamy Peaks and Bigborrowings.

What's that river up there?

The Barrel.

Yes, that's beautiful.

Gorgeous. Take a camera if you go up there. You look directly down the Barrel from Bigborrowings.

Yes. It's lovely country up there.

It's a wonderful place to bring up petrol prices.

Children.

You're telling me.

OK, and you were polled recently?

No, I think that's just these new trousers.

I mean you've been questioned by pollsters.

Yes, sorry, that's correct.

And you've said you believe Peter Costello's version of the meeting with John Howard.

Yes. *(Off.)* Interest rates haven't gone up have they? Still eight per cent?

But you don't want Peter Costello as Prime Minister.

That's right. *(Off.)* Let me know if they go up. They're still eight per cent?

And you've put Kim Beazley ahead of John Howard as preferred Prime Minister.

Yes, that's right.

So if there was an election you'd vote for Kim Beazley.

No we wouldn't. John Howard's the Prime Minister. *(Off.)* Interest rates? Still eight per cent?

So why have you said you'd vote for Kim Beazley?

John Howard's got to know this IR stuff stinks. We're not having that. That's terrible. That's not the way we treat each other in Australia.

Have you said that anywhere here?

Yes.

Where?

We said if there was an election tomorrow we'd vote for Kim Beazley.

What'll you do if interest rates go to ten per cent?

They're not going to do that are they?

I don't know. Nobody can control interest rates.

Give us a ring if interest rates go to ten per cent.

And what'll you do?

I'll tell you what I really think of John Howard.

THE HON. KIM BEAZLEY
LEADER OF THE OPPOSITION

Mr Beazley, thanks for your time.

Very good to be with you, Bryan.

How are things going?

Very well thanks.

Are you busy?

I have been busy.

You're on the road a lot, aren't you?

I am. I've been in Sydney, Brisbane, Melbourne, Canberra.

And are you getting a good response?

By and large, yes. There are critics of course. Not everyone likes it.

There'll always be critics, I suppose.

Exactly. But generally I think things are good.

You're getting good notices in the press.

Yes. You need plenty of coverage. You can build from there.

It's quite an achievement. How do you do it—the John Howard impression? Because you don't look very like him.

No, but I've lost some weight and the John Howard impression's not the only thing I do.

I know but that's what you're best known for. How do you think your way into the character?

I've looked at John Howard for a long time. I studied the way he talks, the sort of things he says, the way he stands.

What sort of things does he say?

He has quite conservative views. He's all for big business. He's a nationalist; he's very big on the army.

Yes, you've caught all those things perfectly.

He's very keen on the popular media; he's on talkback all the time.

Just like you. It really is uncanny.

He gets photographed a lot at sports events.

Yes, he's got that Australian tracksuit.

Yes, the one under his suit?

Yes.

Yes, I've got one on order. He's got a right-wing position on social issues like race and gender, sexuality.

You've got those pretty well now too.

I think the key is to keep expressing a concern for Australian families.

Yes, it's a great smokescreen, isn't it?

It's brilliant. No one knows what it means and I tell you what, when you do it, you can hear a pin drop.

I bet you can. You do it very well. You're very good at that. Have you ever met him, the real John Howard?

Yes, we bump into each other from time to time.

Does he like what you do?

He loves it.

He's a fan?

I saw him this week, Monday I think it was. It was in Adelaide.

What did he say?

He'd seen the thing I'd done on uranium.

Was he nice about it?

He said even he couldn't tell the difference.

High praise. That's great!

He actually congratulated me on it publicly, on Tuesday.

He did. You must be chuffed.

It doesn't get any better than 'I congratulate Mr Beazley on his courageous stand on the question of uranium'.

Mr Howard, thanks for your time.

Ha ha ha ha. Got you there, Bryan.

God he's good.

MR ANDREWS
A CONCERNED PARENT

Mr Andrews, come in.

Thanks.

Please. Take a seat.

Is it about Kevin?

Yes.

I got your message. Is everything OK?

Well, we've just done a big project review. Are you aware of what Kevin was doing?

Well we knew he was working on something. There's a lot of clutter in the house.

It's to prepare them for the sort of task they might be asked to conduct as adults.

Yes, we understand that. It's great training. I don't know about Kevin's project in detail but I actually printed a lot of it out at a work.

OK, well just to put you in the picture, Kevin's taken on industrial reform.

Industrial reform?

You seem surprised.

Yes, don't know why he chose that. What would Kevin know about industrial reform?

I was going to ask you about that.

How did he go?

Well, I think he did a lot of work.

Yes, he did.

Look, to be honest he's got into trouble in couple of key areas. Have a look.

(He reads.) Mmmm. Who are these companies?

They're all companies who don't wish to be associated with Kevin's project.

I'm not surprised. They're dependent on their staff, a lot of these companies. They'll go broke if they introduce…

I'm sure he thought he was helping them.

He hasn't thought this through though, has he? Did you talk to him about this? Has he had help with this?

Yes, I've spent a lot of time with Kevin.

Did he know these companies didn't want a bar of it?

Yes. He said that proved how good the proposal was.

Because these companies wouldn't wear it?

Yes.

Oh dear. *(He reads on.)* Oh God, and he's made it compulsory to dock your own workers' pay if they go to a meeting about it.

Yes, he's actually put them in a difficult position.

Couldn't the staff just say they're not coming in because they got pissed watching the soccer or they've got a pretend cold? Nobody would mind if they didn't come to work.

No, he's painted himself into a bit of corner.

It's all a bit of a mess, isn't it?

Imagine if this were happening in real life.

It'd be hopeless.

Can I ask you something? Is he happy, do you think? Kevin? Is he a happy kid?

I'd describe Kevin as a very normal kid.

Does he have any friends?

He doesn't relax easily socially, I have to say.

Has he ever mentioned John or Philip?

Yes. And Nick, he's got a friend called Nick.

Yes. Is he easily influenced?

This is not the Kevin we know. Is there something we can do at home?

He obviously thinks he's done pretty well with this project.

I think he thinks it's a triumph.

He might need some counselling.

Yes. I might take him camping for a couple of days. Get him out of the house.

Yes, move him round a bit.

Quite a lot I think. I might take the dog. *(He looks again at his son's work.)* Poor bugger. He tried so hard.

THE HON. ALEXANDER DOWNER
MINISTER FOR FOREIGN AFFAIRS

Mr Downer, thank you very much for your time.

It's very good to be with you Bryan, and good evening.

Can you explain to me the legal process we're seeing in the David Hicks trial?

Yes, well Mr Hicks has now of course pleaded guilty to providing material support for a terrorist organisation.

But Mr Downer, wasn't pleading guilty the only way he was going to get home?

Bryan, I would have thought if you plead guilty to something, it's because you did it.

And what if you plead not-guilty?

Well if you're going to lie on oath, Bryan, they're going to chuck the book at you. I wouldn't advise you to do that. That could be dangerous.

OK. So can you explain the legal process to us?

Yes, the auspices here are those of a US constituted military commission. Have you seen the artist's impression drawings that have been in the newspaper?

Yes, and this is David Hicks here.

That's David Hicks there, yes. This is the judge over here.

This is Major Mori?

That's right. Major Mori, yes indeed.

Who's this, here?

That there, Bryan, is the White Rabbit, slightly blurred of course, because he's running late.

Where's Alice?

Alice is over here.

Oh. Behind the Red Queen?

Behind the Red Queen, yes.

Of course. OK. So how does it all work? I mean, this is not coming

under US law is it?

No—it's a slightly different jurisdiction; it's a US military commission, being conducted in a jail in Cuba.

And how is it different?

Well, whereas normally you would be charged with something, and then you would be tried, and then if you were found guilty, you would be sentenced…

Yes. And how is this one different?

In this case, in a slightly different jurisdiction, Bryan, you serve your sentence…

You serve your sentence first?

…and then after some years of that, you're charged, and then perhaps, you're tried.

What are you charged with?

Oh, anything. In this case 'providing material support for a terrorist organisation'.

And where do you serve your sentence?

In a little room about this by this, Bryan. It's very attractive. Affording excellent vistas of the toilet, for example.

And when are you tried?

You're tried after you're charged, as in the conventional model.

Right. And this is after you've served your sentence.

…Having served the majority of your sentence, for some years; maybe five or six years.

And what do you do when you're charged?

Oh you plead guilty, Bryan.

Why do you plead guilty?

Because you've already served your sentence. You don't want to be tried, Bryan, you've probably had enough by then.

Yes. You want to go home.

Time to go home, yes.

The novelty's worn off.

The thrill is gone, Bryan. Let's get out of here.

So why didn't the Australian Government get him out, Mr Downer?

Well, everyone is entitled to a fair trial. That is a fundamental right.

Mr Downer, thanks for your time.

Now you just plead guilty, Bryan and I think I can get you out of here.

THE HON. KEVIN RUDD
LEADER OF THE OPPOSITION

Mr Rudd, thanks for your time.
It's very good to be with you, and thank you for the invitation.
Mr Rudd, you've announced your industrial relations policy this week. I just want to—
Yes we have, Bryan. Do I think we're going to solve all of the problems in one go and do I think this is going to be popular with everybody? No I don't. But do I think it's a better, fairer, more equitable solution for all Australians, Bryan? Yes, I most assuredly do.
Good. Mr Rudd—
Do I think Industrial Relations and Workplace Relations are important, are of the utmost importance in this country? Is that my belief? Yes it most emphatically is. Do I therefore assume that I am simply some sort of Robin Hood who can come along and solve all the problems of the world at a stroke, Bryan? I'll be brutally honest with you. I don't.
No.
No, that is not my view. But am I going to give it a go, Bryan? Am I going to give it a red hot go? Yes, Bryan, that is my belief. That is my commitment. And that is the policy we will be taking to the Australian people.
Yes, Mr Rudd—
We've dropped the ball in this country. We have seriously dropped the ball in this country. We've dropped the ball on global warming. We've dropped the ball on this absolutely ill-advised and doomed war in Iraq. Do I think it's going to be easy to get out of these things, Bryan? I don't.
Probably not, no.
No, I don't. But do I think the Australian public deserves a better go than they're going to get from this bereft, idea-less Howard Government?
Probably, yes.

Absolutely right. Yes I do.

So, Mr Rudd—

Let me ask *you* a question, Bryan. Are we in this country thoroughly sick of being told what the agenda is and told what to think or Bryan do we take the view that we're not children and we don't need to be treated like children?

Yes. Yes we do. But this is not what I asked you, Mr Rudd.

Am I interested in what you ask me, Bryan? Do I look as if I'm interested in what you ask me? Do I look as if I'm yearning for further information about what you actually asked me? Bryan if I were, I'd be answering that question.

Mr Rudd.

And am I doing that? No I'm not.

Well, Mr Rudd, this is not the question I've asked you. I wanted to ask you about AWAs.

Sure. Are we leaving some of the AWAs in place for a very limited period? Yes we are.

(To someone off screen.) **What do I do with this?**

But do we like AWAs? Do we think they're fair? No we most certainly do not. If we don't think they're fair, why are we leaving them in place, Bryan, for a limited period?

Well that's a good question.

That's a *good* question. That's a very good question. I congratulate you on the question. Am I going to answer the question? No I'm not. Is it the right question? No it isn't.

Mr Rudd…

What is the right question? Bryan, that's a very good question. That's an even better question.

I can't do anything here.

Here's another question. Am I a conceited twerp? Bryan, that question is beneath you. You're better than that, Bryan.

Yes.

These are very, very good questions.

He won't shut up.

Very good questions. Should I shut up now? Perhaps I should. In what direction should I shut?

Up.

Correct. What's the capital of Norway?

Oslo.

You're very good, Bryan. Very, very good.

Mr Rudd, thanks for your time.

Oh thank you, Bryan. I loved it. There's nothing I like more than an exchange of ideas.

THE HON. JOHN HOWARD
PRIME MINISTER OF AUSTRALIA

Mr Howard, thanks for your time.

It's a great pleasure to be with you.

I'd like to talk to you about global warming and climate change.

Global warming and climate change?

Yes, what is Australia doing about…

Hang on. (*He is writing it down.*) Global warming.

Global warming and climate change.

Global warming?

Yes, the globe is getting warmer.

When is this going to happen?

It's happening now…

Well, do you want to talk about that as well?

Yes, it's the same thing. Global warming means the globe is warming.

So that's still 'global warming'. We'll cover that under 'global warming' won't we?

Yes. Mr Howard, we've got rising sea levels, climate change, Australia's one of the most affected places on earth.

Sorry, what was the other one? 'Global warming' and what?

Climate change.

(*Writes.*) 'Climate change'?

Yes. The climate is changing. We've just had the hottest October in donkey's years.

(*Writes.*) 'Climate change'.

It's urgent that we do something about all this.

Urgent?

Mr Howard, it was urgent we do something about this ten years ago.

(*Writes.*) 'Urgent'.

Mr Howard…

Hang on, Bryan. How do you spell 'urgent'.

U-r-g-e-n-t.

Looks wrong.

It's right, Mr Howard.

(Writes again.) 'Urgent'.

Yes, Mr Howard what is the Australian Government doing to ensure that…

Bryan, I'm trying to get all this down so we can discuss it. 'Urgent'.

Yes. Looks better in capitals.

Mr Howard.

Right. Global warming. Climate change. And it's urgent.

It was urgent ten years ago.

Is it still urgent?

Yes.

We'll cover that under 'urgency'. Anything else?

No. Mr Howard, what is Australia doing about climate change and global warming?

Climate change and global warming?

Yes

Hang on. I've got them the wrong way round. Is it still urgent?

Yes.

Can we have some water?

We haven't got any water.

Don't be silly, Bryan.

THE HON. PAUL LENNON
PREMIER OF TASMANIA

Premier Lennon, thanks for your time.

Good evening Bryan, very good to be with you.

As Premier, I'd like to talk to you about Tasmania.

Yes, well, I'm always very happy to talk about Tasmania, a great place, Tasmania, Bryan, very happy to talk about it. What particular aspect of it interests you?

Well, the administration, how it all works. You run the government, is that right?

Sure, Bryan. Do you want to talk about the people who run Tasmania or do you want to talk about the government?

Well…they're different?

Yes. We've got a bicameral system.

Yes, two houses, sure.

No, there are plenty of houses, Bryan, it's just that we got a bicameral system of administration in Tasmania.

What are they?

 Well, I'm the government…

The administration of the state, yes…

… I'm very happy to talk to you about the government, Bryan, I'm the Premier. It's quite interesting. It's very interesting work. You need a suit and a tie, a fax machine…

A what?

A fax machine, you need a fax machine.

A fax machine. Why?

Well, they're going to need to get in contact with you, aren't they, the people who need the laws passed.

But don't you write the laws?

No, no, we *pass* the laws. It's a bicameral system.

Well who writes it?

I don't know who writes them, Bryan. We just get them off a fax machine and we bung them through the Parliament.

You just pass them?

Yes, all those in favour go through that door or that door. It's a bit like panto. We quite enjoy it. It's a beautiful building the Parliament. Pop in if you're in the area.

You're saying the government is different from the administration, is that right?

Bryan, what I'm saying is we pass the laws.

So who runs the state?

I run the state. I'm the CEO of Gunns.

No, hang on, you're the Premier of Tasmania.

Sorry, no, I beg your pardon. The guy who runs the state is the CEO of Gunns, I'm just the Premier.

Right. Is Gunns your electorate?

Oh, Gunns is everybody's electorate, Bryan. You're mad if you're not in the Gunns electorate.

You're the Premier of Tasmania?

That's right, that's my job.

You were elected?

That's right. By Gunns. They put me there and I'm doing the job as well as I possibly can.

Who are Gunns?

Gunns are the people who make the laws in Tasmania in the bicameral system I'm trying to explain to you.

Well what are the laws about?

Anything. A lot of Tasmanian laws are about trees.

What about trees?

Oh, where they are…

…How to get to them?

…How to get them out.

Yes. What happens to the trees when you get them out?

They sell them. They're sold. They make them into paper.

Paper?

Yes. Make them into paper.

What for?

So we can get the faxes off the fax machine, Bryan, you can't get the fax off the fax machine if there's no paper in the fax machine.

So they make fax paper out of these things?

That's right. Exactly. Get the trees out, turn them into fax paper.

So really, this is all about chopping trees down?

Well, the trees aren't going to walk out themselves and turn themselves into fax paper, are they? You've got to chop them down.

Are you familiar with global warming?

No, who does he work for? Get him to call me; I'll be in the Parliament.

Mr Lennon, thanks for your time.

Is that a Gunns' fax?

No, no.

'Thanks for your time'. I get a few saying, 'Thanks for your time' from Gunns, that's all.

Oh do you? They thank you?

Yes, course they do. I'm the Premier of the state.

Yes, but they run it.

It's a bicameral system, yes.

Two cameras.

Yes, just like here.

Yes, good.

(Grabs Bryan's question sheet.) Give me that, I'll make it into a law.

Kevin Rudd

Kevin Rudd (born 21 September 1957) was a notably precocious child; at the age of three he was taught Greek. By the age of six he had read Aesop's *Fables*, Xenophon's *Anabasis,* and the whole of Herodotus, and was acquainted with Lucian, Diogenes Laërtius, Isocrates and six dialogues of Plato. He had also read a great deal of history in English and had been taught arithmetic.

At the age of eight he began learning Latin, Euclid, algebra and Mandarin Chinese.

His main reading was history, but he also went through Horace, Virgil, Ovid, Tacitus, Homer, Dionysus, Sophocles, Euripides, Aristophanes and Thucydides. By the age of ten he could read Plato and Demosthenes with ease. One of Kevin's earliest poetry compositions was a continuation of the *Iliad*. In his spare time, he also enjoyed reading about natural sciences and popular novels, such as *Don Quixote* and *Robinson Crusoe*.

Rudd became Prime Minister of Australia on 3 December 2007.

The term **Kevinrudd** (from German: 'miracle child' or 'wonder child') is sometimes used as a synonym for **prodigy**, particularly in media accounts, although this term is discouraged in scientific literature. *Kevinrudds* are often those who achieve success and acclaim early in their adult careers, such as Steven Spielberg, Steve Jobs and Michael Jackson.

THE HON. KEVIN RUDD
LEADER OF THE OPPOSITION

Mr Rudd, thanks for coming in.

Very good to be with you, Bryan, and good evening.

How was the policy launch?

Yesterday went very well thank you, a few technical glitches but we got through them.

It was like a rock concert reception?

We got a great result, it was a fantastic, stadium rock quality occasion, yes.

The campaign's been going for a while now, hasn't it?

Yes, four years on Tuesday, Bryan.

Really, four years?

Yes, indeed.

So, who's been running the country while this is all happening?

I imagine Paul Kelly.

From the *Australian*?

Yes, he's the only one with both the knowledge and with the practical experience.

Of running a country.

Of running a country.

So, what would he do if something went wrong?

Ring Glenn Milne I suppose.

There's been criticism you're running a 'me too' campaign?

There has been, yes, but that's not what we do. We're not doing that. There are significant differences between the two parties, we're asking people to make a choice.

Mr Rudd, that is nonsense. You're saying exactly the same thing.

We're not, Bryan, you've misread that, that's not what we do.

(Bryan's mobile phone rings.) **Hello? Yes, thanks for calling.** Who's that?

It's John Howard, he's ringing to agree with you.

Well, of course he would, Bryan, because…

He's saying exactly the same thing over the telephone as you say everywhere.

That's not right.

He wants to talk to you. *(Passes the mobile phone.)*

Hello, John? I agree with you, exactly. I'm with you all the way. Yes, well exactly. I've just been…No, couldn't have put it better myself. Could not agree more. Pardon? Paul Kelly, yes. Glenn Milne, I suppose. No, I'll give you back to Bryan. Pardon? No, I think it will be close, too. Yes, I agree, very close indeed. *(Passes the mobile phone to Bryan Dawe.)*

Hello? Yes, I know you think it will be close, Mr Howard.

I've got to shift my car.

No, Kevin's just going to go and shift his car. John's just shifting his car too.

There you go. Clear choice.

THE HON. BRENDAN NELSON
LEADER OF THE OPPOSITION

Brendan Nelson, thanks for your time.

Good evening Bryan, it's very good of you to invite me on the program.

Congratulations on the leadership.

Thank you very much. Thank you very much.

How have you been enjoying it?

I'm loving it, Bryan. It's a great honour. It's a big job, no question, and I'm conscious of a great deal of responsibility.

Yes, you've had this ambition for a long while, haven't you?

I think everybody who goes into politics, deep down harbours a secret desire to… *(Bryan is distracted.)* What's the problem, Bryan?

Hang on. Sorry, there's a big shadow over you.

A big shadow over me?

Why is there a big shadow over Dr Nelson?

I can move, Bryan.

No, no. But it goes with you.

It goes with me? What? It came in with me?

Yes, I saw it when you came in.

Well that's a bit of a shame, Bryan. I thought the interview was going particularly well…

We'll try and fix it. It'll be OK.

…On the subject of my leadership.

We'll fix it.

Good.

It is a strange time for the party isn't it?

It is a strange time. But we were in government for a very long period of time, Bryan.

(Shadow lifts slightly.)

Oh there we go, that's better.

There's a lot of experience in the party, Bryan. So we'll be back.

And then there was the drubbing, wasn't there?

What drubbing? I wouldn't characterise what happened in the election as a drubbing, Bryan.

Come on, Dr Nelson. Please. The Prime Minister lost his seat.

The view of the Australian people was expressed with particular clarity, Bryan, in the Bennelong area but…

And the Treasurer then melted off into the night. Is that a success of some kind?

Look, I'm not saying it's a good result. I wouldn't characterise it as a success.

Well how would you characterise the result?

I suppose a drubbing is probably the correct term, Bryan.

I wasn't trying to be rude. I mean call it a defeat if you would like— that's fine.

No, no, I take your point, Bryan, we were thrashed. We got thumped. And there are lessons there. And we've got to learn those lessons. I'm very conscious of that.

So what do you think your leadership offers the party?

Well, I suppose the obvious thing to say here, Bryan, is generational change. The Prime Minister was in office for a very long…

(Shadow has fallen again.)

Oh hang on a minute.

What's the problem here, Bryan?

Sorry, Dr Nelson. Why is there a dirty big shadow over the top of Dr Nelson? Please! I'm trying to interview the man about leadership.

Bryan, I can't see a shadow.

Well it's there.

I don't think there is a shadow here, Bryan.

You can't see it, but it's there.

I don't think it's here, Bryan. I'm talking about leadership and there is no shadow that I'm aware of.

It's there. Trust me.

Generational change was what I was talking about, Bryan.

Yes. OK. Talk about generational change.

The National Party and the Liberal Party have recently undertaken generational change. Although we at the Liberal Party of course, have gone younger.

And what did the National Party do?

In the case of the National Party, Mr Vaile has stood aside for an older man. That's a slightly different approach.

So what will your leadership seek to do with the party?

We need to rebuild the party. Let's be very clear about this. We need to rebuild…

(Shadow falls again.)

Oh no, not again. Hang on.

Is that the same problem? I know what this will be, Bryan. Just sit still. I'll fix this. *(Calls off.)* Malcolm? Can you bugger off? I mean for heaven's sake, I'm doing an interview. I've told you about this before. I'll come and talk to you outside afterwards. Please just go away.

Who's the little guy with the ears?

No idea. Just get outside! I'm talking about leadership.

(Off.) **Could you please just go away? I'm trying to interview the man about leadership.**

That's right, leadership. It's very, very important.

Yes.

(The lights go out.)

Whoops!

Oh no. This is ridiculous. Has anyone here got a torch, please?

It's all right, Bryan, it's all right. *(Lights a cigarette lighter.)* I'm very anxious to continue, talk about leadership. Go on. Ask me about leadership. I'm pretty good on this—it's my special subject.

THE HON. PETER GARRETT
MINISTER FOR THE ENVIRONMENT,
HERITAGE AND THE ARTS

Peter Garrett, thanks for your time.
Good evening, Bryan, very good to be with you.
You've been stripped of your responsibilities?
No, no, nobody's been stripped of their responsibilities in the environmental area. We're all going to be responsible.
Well, you have.
No, I know what you mean but no, that's a misreading. Kevin has made me the minister in the area of my particular special interest.
Yes, but you're not allowed to talk about it.
Yes, I am. I just won't be answering questions about it in the Parliament.
Why on earth not?
Because the meta issues, the economics and the planning, they are all the province of other ministries. And the people with carriage of that will be answering those questions. That's logical.
Who are they?
They are Wayne Swan in the lower house and Penny Wong in the Senate.
What would Wayne Swan know about the environment?
The point I'm making is that he has carriage of those meta issues and he will be answering those questions.
What is your portfolio then?
I'm the Minister for the Environment.
And what is your area of expertise?
The environment, Bryan. That's why I'm the minister.
Brendan Nelson says he finds it extraordinary that the environment spokesman will not be asked questions about climate change. It's a fair question.
I'm not surprised Brendan finds a few things fairly extraordinary at the moment. Is he still the leader incidentally?

Yes, I think so.

It's the first time they've elected a leader who was previously a member of our party. I'm not surprised he's got a few perceptual struggles at the moment.

Sure. So, Mr Garrett, what you're saying is you're the minister for not saying anything about the environment? Is that right?

Or climate change, Bryan.

Yes. Can you say anything about any other portfolios?

Well, obviously the environment and climate change are my particular areas of expertise.

The areas you won't be answering questions about?

That's as I understand it, yes.

So, should you be answering these questions? I don't want you to be in trouble.

Now? No, no, I'll be OK now, Bryan, as long as I'm home by ten.

Are you sure? Are there any other ministers specifically excluded from answering questions about the thing they're ministers for?

It's a bit early for that, Bryan. We've only been in office for a minute.

Are you a minister without portfolio?

I'm not a minister without portfolio, no. I have a portfolio.

But you're not the minister for speaking about it.

Yes I am.

Are you the spokesman for it?

Yes, indeed I am, Bryan.

So, what are you allowed to say about it?

That's the area of some uncertainty just at the minute.

You'd need to check?

That's what I'd need to check, yes.

But why would you need to check it?

So I don't put someone in a difficult position, if they've got responsibility for answering questions in the Parliament about my portfolio.

Mr Garrett, are you happy about this?

I'm very happy about it, Bryan. I think it'll work well. And I have great respect for both usurpers and bugger it.

(Correcting him.) **For both ministers and Mr Rudd?**

Yes, sorry, you're quite right. Can't read my own writing.

Mr Garrett, thanks for your time.

Sorry, Kevin.

THE HON. WAYNE SWAN
TREASURER

Wayne Swan, thanks for your time tonight.
Pleasure.
You're bringing down your first federal Budget on Tuesday.
That's right.
Peter Costello not available?
Peter's no longer with the firm.
Really. Where's Peter gone?
I don't know what Peter's doing now.
You miss him?
No we got him.
There's a lot of speculation about what's in the Budget, isn't there?
I hope so. I'm doing everything possible to…
And the opposition says you're trying to create an inflation crisis.
Yes, they do. They're not very bright, the opposition.
Are you trying to create an inflation crisis?
We don't need to create one. We've got one. And by doing nothing for ten years they helped develop it.
What is an inflation crisis?
Inflation means prices are going up.
And are likely to keep going up…
Yes.
In the future…
Going forward.
Pardon?
You don't say 'in the future'. You say 'going forward'. We say 'going forward'.
'Going forward'.
Yes. What you're talking about there is prices trending northward 'going forward'.
What does that mean?
It means prices are going up.

And likely to keep increasing.

Yes, that would be the fear.

Going forward.

In the future, yes.

Because the price of petrol has gone up.

Yes.

And the price of food.

Yes, the price of water's gone up.

So they're not coming down.

Going forward?

Yes.

We don't think so.

So how do you prevent inflation?

There are two ways, fiscal and monetary. Fiscal is to do with
government expenditure and monetary is to do with the money supply.

If the government spends less doesn't that reduce the money supply?

Yes, and there has been a series of interest rate rises to try to put the
brakes on spending.

So prices don't run away?

Correct.

Don't increased interest rates contribute to inflation?

Yes, that's the legacy of the Howard Government. That's why we're
reducing government spending.

To reduce the money supply?

Exactly.

Won't that make it harder for people to get money?

It will, yes.

What about the price of food and petrol?

Exactly.

I mean going forward.

No. No one will be going forward. You won't be able to go anywhere.

This is going forward.

No, you won't be able to go anywhere.

I mean in the future.

You mean after Tuesday?

Yes.

So do I, Bryan.

KEVIN RUDD'S FATHER
A CONCERNED PARENT

Thanks for coming in.

That's all right. Is it about Kevin?

It is about Kevin but it's not *all* about Kevin.

Have you told Kevin that? I'm pretty sure he thinks it's all about...

I wanted to have this conversation with you first.

Is he going all right?

Kevin's going very well. We're very pleased with him.

He's very pleased with himself.

He should be. He's going well.

Yes he tells us he's going well.

When does he sleep, Kevin?

We don't know. We thought he must be sleeping at school.

No he's not sleeping here. He came back from this geography trip and...

Yes, we're knee-deep in postcards.

And he ran a big conference.

Yes, he's very keen. He loves all the activities.

Yes. Now, there's a boy here, a new boy, who's a bit lost.

That's no good.

He's maybe a bit out of his depth. Having trouble fitting in.

I'm sorry to hear that.

We wonder if Kevin could play a role here.

Yes, I'm sure he could. I'm sure he'd be good at it.

The boy's name is Brendan.

Oh Brendan? With the haircut?

Yes, I wonder if Kevin could take him under his wing a bit.

We know Brendan.

How do you know Brendan?

He comes home with Kevin sometimes. He follows him home. Kevin took him to the conference didn't he?

He did.

Yes. Kevin did his homework one night.

Did he? What homework?

Aboriginal history.

Yes, Brendan did quite well in that.

Yes he did.

He got second.

Yes. Kevin got first I think.

Yes he did. So you know Brendan?

Yes, we see him a bit. Kevin says Brendan's friends aren't very nice to him.

That's right, that's very perceptive of Kevin.

Although Brendan's imaginary friend is nice to him.

Brendan has an imaginary friend?

Yes.

And his imaginary friend is nice to him.

Yes.

Well that's nice, if his real friends aren't being nice to him.

Yes, it's good.

And who is Brendan's imaginary friend?

Kevin.

Are you sure Kevin doesn't sleep at home?

No. He's always working on some project. He's just finished one.

What was it?

Governor-General. Beautiful new Governor-General. Pink raffia work.

THE HON. KEVIN RUDD
PRIME MINISTER OF AUSTRALIA

Kevin Rudd, good evening.

Good evening Bryan.

Now, you've announced you're having a summit meeting with a number of very prominent Australians.

Yes, and some not very prominent ones.

Yes, because the government will be there, won't they?

Yes, I meant there'll be a lot of ordinary people there as well.

Yes, the federal ministers will all be in attendance won't they?

Yes, the point I'm making is that a great many people who aren't in politics at all will be at the…

At the talkfest.

At the ideas summit. It's not a talkfest Bryan. It's an ideas summit.

Mr Rudd. Hasn't the country just voted for you on the basis of the ideas you put before the electorate?

It has but before embarking on this great adventure into the future we want to get the benefit of the best ideas in the country.

Rather than your own.

As well as our own.

So you've got a few?

We're knee-deep in them down at the institute, yes. We'll be priming the pump with a few of our own ideas.

And then the others will follow.

They will, as the night the day.

How have you selected the people who'll be there?

We've tried to attract a broad range of people with a wide spectrum of expertise and most importantly of course, people with ideas.

What sort of ideas will they bring to the table?

We won't know till they get there but I think there are going to be some very good ideas.

It's in April, isn't it?

It is, yes.

Is that a particularly good time for ideas, is it? April?

It's a particularly propitious period for ideas, yes.

Why is that?

I don't know. That's an interesting question.

Will you bring that up?

I could bring that up, yes.

Yes, I'd like to know.

We might start off with that one. That could get things going nicely.

Do you think this is anything like Mr Hawke's great whatever it was...

Talkfest.

Wasn't Mr Hawke's an ideas summit?

At the time they thought it was but no, it's not similar except in the sense that it's an ecumenical, broad, very inclusive and very wide-ranging...

Talkfest.

Ideas summit.

And you expect it to come up with some ideas?

I'm sure it will.

Why?

I know what some of them are going to say.

What are they going to say?

They're going to say it's great to have an ideas summit.

Where are they going to say this?

At the talkfest.

THE HON. PHILIP RUDDOCK
FORMER ATTORNEY-GENERAL

Mr Ruddock, thank you for coming in.

It has been too long, Bryan.

You've expressed regret this week.

I have, yes.

About the length of time the Australian Government held children in detention.

That's right.

This was when you were in government?

Yes, that's right.

What was your portfolio at the time?

I was the immigration minister.

And who were the children?

They were the children of people seeking asylum in Australia.

And they were put in detention?

Yes.

Is that normal?

It was normal at that time.

And you now regret that?

I regret the length of time the children were kept in detention.

Yes, and did you speak to the immigration minister?

I was the immigration minister.

So you regret yourself?

I do not regret myself. I regret that the children were not released earlier than they were.

Why weren't the children released earlier?

Because of a lack of funding.

Are there hidden costs in opening a gate?

That is a facetious remark and one I am inclined to ignore.

Well, you tell me, what are the costs in letting children out of a jail?

It was not a jail.

What was it called then, this place where children were incarcerated

for longer than you now think they should have been?

The children, as I have repeatedly said, were in detention.

And you would have liked extra funding for what reason?

I said I regret that we did not have extra funding.

Why?

We could have built a better jail.

For the children?

A jail more suitable for the retention of children.

Maybe with some toys?

What are toys?

You've also expressed some misgivings about the handling of the Haneef case.

There was no case against Mr Haneef.

That's right. No case was brought against Dr Haneef. You have some concerns about the handling of the matter.

There was an investigation by the police and another by ASIO and the legal view may be that each of these compromises the other.

And did you speak to the Attorney-General?

I was the Attorney-General.

Will we be hearing more of your regrets?

I imagine I might have further regrets, yes, over time.

As you think about what you did?

I do not regret what I did.

You did everything you've regretted so far.

I regret the circumstances in which I was forced to do these things.

For eleven years.

For eleven years.

Thanks for your time.

I shot the albatross.